Dressmaking
with
Leather

To W.O.G.

By the same author
Take Half-a-Yard of Fabric
Knowing Your Sewing
Knowing Your Dressmaking

Dressmaking with Leather

Maureen Goldsworthy
M.A. (Cantab.), Honours Diploma, Leather Institute

B T Batsford Limited
London

ISBN 0 7134 3240 3

Filmset by Servis Filmsetting Ltd, Manchester
Printed by The Anchor Press Ltd, Tiptree, Essex
for the Publishers B T Batsford Limited
4 Fitzhardinge Street, London W1H 0AH

Contents

ACKNOWLEDGMENTS

During the preparation of this book, I have been most grateful for the kindness shown and the help so freely given to me by many people and organizations. I should like particularly to thank Mrs Betty Townsend, of the Mid-Warwickshire College of Further Education, who designed, made and modelled the clothes shown in Plate 3, and page 90. My warm thanks go also to Miss Juliet Powell-Brett, Mr Frederick Ellis, Mr Ben Phillips and to my daughter Alice, who modelled the other garments; to Mr and Mrs A.B. Measures, for allowing the clothes to be photographed in their beautiful riverside garden; and above all to Vicky Carter, for her luminous photography and artistic judgment. On the technical side, I should first acknowledge my indebtedness (as must anyone, writing about any aspect of leather) to that great work of reference, *Leather: in Life, Art and Industry* by John W. Waterer. I am deeply grateful to those who have been kind enough to read parts of the text; to Mr David Tuck, A.L.C., vice-principal of the National Leathersellers College, for giving me the benefit of his wide knowledge of the history, structure and processing of leather; to Margaret Hanson of The Leather Shop, Warwick, for making valuable suggestions on the manufacture of garments; and to Mr Henry Bristow, A.G.C.L., for information on dry-cleaning. My thanks are also due to Miss Jocelyn Morris, F.S.A., director of Warwickshire Museum Services, and to Miss Barbara Clayton, Keeper of Archaeology, for their help and advice in research; to Mr William Cox of the Leather Institute for much practical help; to Mr Richard Draper, managing director of R.J. Draper & Co. Ltd, who was kind enough to let me study, under the guidance of Mrs Sylvia Appleby, the methods used in his factory; to Clark, Son & Morland Ltd; to C.W. Pittard & Co. Ltd; to Mr A. Saunders of Midland Sewing Machines Ltd, particularly for advice on threads; to Mr L.A. Jordan of The Castle Cleaners, Warwick, for his help in testing the suitability for dry-cleaning of various paints, dyes and adhesives; to Miss Caroline Hampton for information on the home tanning of sheepskins, and to Mrs E.A.T. MacEwen, Isle of Muck, for the recipes.

The photographs of leather structure on pages 18, 19, 22 and 39 are reproduced by courtesy of the British Leather Manufacturers' Research Association; the photograph on page 12 by courtesy of The Museum of Leathercraft, Walsall; and the photograph on Plate 1 by courtesy of The Board of Trinity College, Dublin.

INTRODUCTION

Although leather has been used by man since the earliest times, only recently has it become a high fashion material. The traditional methods of tanning and finishing produced heavy, thick leathers with little stretch or drape – and in dark or dull colours. Leather coats used to be stiff, substantial and mannish in character. Sheepskins used to be heavy; they certainly lasted almost for ever, but were serviceable rather than elegant. Being so thick, leather was not an easy material to make up, nor had it enough fashion appeal to tempt home dressmakers to try their hand. Superb, perhaps, for shoes or handbags, but not for clothes. Gloves, of course, were always made from the finer leathers or suèdes; but they needed dry-cleaning, and with the older, vegetable dyestuffs they tended to lose their original colour or went patchy.

Now, however, new methods of dyeing can give the whole range of colours – pastel or dark, delicate or rich, bright or subtle, even dazzling white – and all the colours are fast. New chemical methods of tanning have made leather finer, lighter in weight and more supple. It drapes beautifully, is never restricting but moulds itself to the body, stretching and regaining its shape almost as it did on the animal that first wore it. It is utterly comfortable, as nature designed it to be.

Just as important, the new leathers are easy-care. They can be dry-cleaned and many can be washed in perfect safety, without losing any of their character or suppleness. So at last a leather or suède garment is neither a problem nor an impractical extravagance. In fact, it should last longer than a similar garment made from cloth, while looking, all its life, much more elegant and luxurious.

Leather 'breathes' – its structure enables it to absorb dampness and trap air between its fibres, so it is comfortable to wear, and never clammy like plastic. Being both rain-proof and wind-proof, it is ideal for outdoors. Warm without being bulky, it makes up into very slimming garments. Add to all these qualities the soft velvety surface of suède, or the grain pattern and rich sheen of leather, and it is easy to see why leather clothes are now making such an impact on fashion.

At first sight, leather may seem expensive to make up, as there is so much waste from the shape of the skins. But in fact jackets, waistcoats and skirts (not to mention shirts and blouses made from the finer skins) work out at no more than one would expect to pay for ready-made fabric garments of comparable quality. As the price of woollen cloth rises, the differential becomes smaller.

Neither should one be put off by thinking that leather must be difficult to sew. It is just quite *different* from fabric, needing different methods and techniques, and using such diverse aids as hammers and adhesives, spring-clips and masking-tape. But the home dressmaker cannot simply copy the standard practices used in leather garment manufacture, as many of these are inappropriate for domestic sewing machines. So new techniques are still being evolved. In this book, I offer those methods which I find work most reliably with different types of leather. Because it is not a standard product, there is not always a standard answer to a problem; one should keep an open mind and be prepared to experiment. More sympathetic than any fabric, leather by its very feel and handle can often indicate a suitable – and sometimes novel – solution.

As an amateur, one cannot compete with the specialist manufacturer in producing beautifully tailored coats from the heavier skins; but in those of lighter weight, one can make elegant, well-fitting garments of great style and individuality. This book aims to show how anyone reasonably good at dressmaking can be equally successful with leather.

About Leather

Leather, the first raw material used by man, can be made from the skin of almost any mammal, reptile or bird. The earliest uses for leather, before the weaving of textiles, must have been those needing a two-dimensional material, both flexible and of considerable size. In temperate and cold climates, there was virtually no such material, other than the skins and hides of animals. So it is fair to assume that the early hunting, nomadic tribes must have used skins to satisfy the widest possible variety of needs.

There is even evidence of flint tools, dating from before the Great Ice Age, more than a million years ago, which may have been used by primitive man to scrape the flesh from the hides of animals. These were not leather, of course; they would have been raw and putrescent, discarded when they disintegrated. Later, men learned to stretch out skins for the sun to dry and harden; and then softened them by rubbing with animal brains, which provided fat and oil to make them supple.

Vegetable tanning is the process of treating skins with a liquor of tannin or tannic acid, which is present in the bark of some trees, such as oak and sumach, and in some seed pods. It changes protein into a substance that resists decomposition; soaking skins in pits filled with this liquor produced the first true leather which, after treating with tallow and oil, became both pliable and stable against bacteria.

Leather was used to make tents and give shelter, for clothing and footwear, beds and boats, bottles and containers, harnesses and armour. Decorated leather harnesses for oxen and asses, dating from 3500 BC, have been discovered in the Royal Tombs at Ur of the Chaldees.

The oldest portable records were written on parchment, made from the dried and stretched but untanned skins of sheep. Vellum, originally the skin of new-born calves, gave an even finer white membrane. These materials are extremely durable. An Egyptian mathematical roll made of goatskin (now in the British Museum), retained enough of its original resilience to make it possible for the folds, bound in for the best part of 4,000 years, to be relaxed and flattened, and its contents deciphered – including an error in the addition of fractions. Teachers made mistakes even then, but it is hard to be caught out after such a respectable interval.

Just as extraordinary is the superb condition of early Christian manuscripts, such as the eighth-century Book of Kells, with its intricate, fantastic illumination, and the earlier and even more astonishing Book of Durrow, a folio of which is shown in Plate 1. This seventh-century gospel manuscript may have been written either at Iona or at the monastery of Durrow, County Meath, where it was kept until the seventeenth century. After the dissolution of that monastery, the Book of Durrow, already 1,000 years old, came into the hands of a family who habitually soaked it in their cattle troughs to make holy the water, and so to cure the sicknesses of the beasts that drank it. Even after such treatment, continuing over many years, the colours of the illuminated pages are still as fresh and enamel-brilliant as if they had just been applied.

In mediaeval Spain, a process known as 'tawing' – treating with a strong solution of alum and salt – was used to produce fine, soft, white leathers from goat and kidskin. These, dyed scarlet or other brilliant colours, often decorated with gold, were the most prized leathers of their time, in demand all over Europe for shoes, hangings and upholstery. Their disadvantage was that they were not at all resistant to water. Cordova, the centre of this trade, gave its name to Cordovan leather, and thus indirectly to our own Guild of Cordwainers.

Heavier leathers were used for every kind of container, from large coffers and chests, to bottles. In England, leather bottles were keg-shaped (rather like stone hot-water bottles), sewn with the grain side out, and lined with pitch. Some were probably cured by hanging them in the smoke over wood fires, in much the same way as 'green' bacon was smoked. The old song, 'Ten Green Bottles', refers to this curing of skin bottles from the green or raw state. Some bottles were apparently used for

irregular purposes. Thomas Tusser, the poet and farmer of Tudor times, warned against the 'pilfering thresher' who:

'In his bottle of leather so great,
Will carry home, daily, both barley and wheat'.

This bottle must have been of considerable size to make the pilfering worth-while.

Ale was drunk from tankard-shaped black jacks, also uniquely English, made from two pieces of hide – one for the bottom and one forming the sides and handle of the jack. Sometimes they were given handsome silver mounts, as shown here. It is sung of Simon the Cellarer:

'Yo-ho! Yo-ho! His nose doth show
How oft the black jack to his lips doth go'.

(Figure 1)

Cromwell's soldiers wore long, heavy buff leather coats, a full quarter-inch thick, as a protective layer under the cuirass, itself a word derived from *cuir* – leather. Even after the Industrial Revolution, leather played a major part in all kinds of equipment. There was still no better material for transmission belting, for bellows, or for covering the rollers of textile machinery. Stage coaches needed leather suspension – even railways used leather for upholstery, hinges, water-hoses and the corridor screens between coaches.

That great engineer and inventor, Isambard Kingdom Brunel, used leather flanges to seal the vacuum 'rail' of his experimental atmospheric railway (the fastest of its day, reaching 80 mph), where the motive power was provided by stationary steam engines beside the line, drawing the train along by means of a vacuum tube. Unfortunately, Dorset rats, attracted by the leather flanges – or perhaps by the grease that covered them – nibbled, and broke the vacuum. It is startling to visulize (had plastics been available to Brunel) a fast, silent Great Western Railway system with pumping stations but no locomotives.

Even today, the industrial uses of leather, which nothing else can efficiently replace, range from washers, gaskets, and packings in machinery and ships' steering gear controls, to pump cups for oil extraction. Its domestic uses are for shoes, clothing, gloves, upholstery, bags, travel goods and sports equipment.

figure 1
Leather bottle and black jack (Courtesy of the Museum of Leathercraft, Walsall).

TYPES OF LEATHER

The larger the animal, the thicker tends to be its skin. The differences in structure and thickness have always determined the different uses to which the various kinds of leather have been put. In addition, different methods of tanning and finishing can give quite dissimilar properties of handle, softness, texture and drape to skins that were originally alike.

Nappa and suède

To begin with the most obvious point, leather has an outside and an inside. The 'grain' side formed the outer skin of the animal, and this grain shows the root pattern of the hair or wool. In clothing leathers it is given a soft, waxy resin finish, and is known as *nappa*. If the reverse side is finished, it becomes *suède* – so called because it was first used in Sweden for gloves (*gants de Suède*). These terms are usually qualified by a reference to the original animal, such as 'bovine nappa' or 'pigskin suède', etc.

Hides, kips and skins

Animals' skins are flayed from the carcass by making the first cut along the mid-belly line; so all skins, of whatever size, have much the same characteristic shape. Their sizes, however, are so disparate that different terms are used to describe them. *(Figure 2)*

Hides are over 25 square feet in area, and come mainly from cattle, but also from such exotic animals as buffalo, elephant, kangaroo and walrus.

Kips are from 15 to 25 square feet, and include the hides of small Indian cattle.

Skins are smaller than 15 square feet, and comprise sheep, goat, pig and calf. The measurement into square feet includes the whole of the leather surface, faults, edges and all, whether or not it is all usable.

Oxhide and cowhide

These have always been used for the heaviest applications, such as shoe soles. But they are far too stiff and heavy to use for clothing in their entire thickness, and are therefore split into two layers during processing: the *grain split*, which is the top layer of the leather, and the *flesh split*, or under layer.

The grain split is used for shoe uppers and also for clothing. The flesh split makes a suède with a long, rather rough nap; it is thicker and cheaper than the grain split, but its dye is sometimes suspect. For clothing, these leathers are produced in thicknesses between 0.7 and 0.9 mm. Sometimes the hide may be split into three layers, making thinner grain and flesh splits, and giving a third or middle split – not as strong as either of the others. It is often used for teenage garments in the cheaper price ranges, but tends to stretch out of shape or even to disintegrate into holes when given hard wear. It is not worth putting good work into middle splits; but when you are buying, they are unfortunately not easy to distinguish from flesh splits.

Not all hides and skins are suitable for use as leather. Lowest grade hides are made into glues and gelatine; and poor quality skins, although one hates to think of it, into sausage casings.

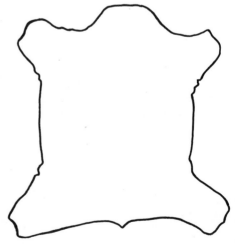

figure 2

Calf

This is more flexible than the hides from adult cattle, and may be used for clothing, accessories and upholstery as well as for shoe uppers. The flesh split, or the reverse of the grain split, treated to resemble buckskin, is used for shoes and clothing. A calf skin is from 6 square feet upwards.

Sheepskins

These form the basis of the modern leather clothing industry in this country. They are extremely versatile, as they can be produced in a wide range of thicknesses from 0.5 to 0.9 mm, with very good qualities of drape and surface texture. In addition to clothing leathers, there are fine gloving nappas and suèdes, which are washable; also the light-weight shirt-suèdes.

Nappas and suèdes from sheep are not split, but use the whole thickness of the skins. The exception is where skins are vegetable-tanned especially for fine book binding skivers. The flesh splits from these skins are 'shamoyed', a form of tannage using fish or whale oil, to become chamois leather. It is actually the oxidization of the oil, with heat, which tans the skin. The characteristics of chamois, of course, are its pale yellow colour, its softness and its capacity for coming up as good as new after innumerable washings.

Different breeds of sheep, from varying climates, each have their own characteristics. The very finest nappas and suèdes are the East India skins (also known as Persians), which come from hair sheep – hardly distinguishable from goats – and which are mostly tanned by vegetable processes in southern India. These skins are small, though, and are not as widely used as the Cape nappas and suèdes from South Africa, which have the largest skin area, up to 12 square feet; or the Cabrettas from South America and from East and West Africa. They are fine-grained, tight-textured and supple, and are used for clothing and gloves. Smaller than these are the domestic nappas and suèdes, averaging between 6 and 7 square feet (about 2.5 feet long), from sheep reared in Great Britain; these, with skins from other temperate countries, make up the bulk of the clothing leathers used here.

Sheepskins can also, of course, be dressed with the wool on; either leaving it long, as in beaver or lucca lamb, or sheared to a wool length of 1 to 2 cm ($\frac{1}{2}$ in. to $\frac{3}{4}$ in.), in which case they are known as shearlings. The skins are suèded on the flesh side, and usually made up with the wool on the inside of the garment. Lambskins are similar to shearlings, but have finer skins and curlier, softer wool. The most suitable breeds of sheep for shearlings are the coarse-woolled hill sheep from temperate climates, either domestic or from New Zealand. They produce a better suède side than the heavily-woolled merino sheep; while breeds from warmer climates may have hair too coarse and sparse to give a satisfactory wool texture.

An entirely new development, pioneered by Clark, Son & Morland Ltd, is a material known as Wolfix. In searching for a use for the fleeces discarded from shearling skins, they invented an ingenious method of securing a fabric backing to the cut side of the fleece. To look at, the fleece is indistinguishable from one on its own skin, and it is dyed in the normal way; however, it can not only be washed, but even boiled and sterilized. There is a growing medical need for such fleeces; and because of their light weight and easy-care properties, one hopes to see them becoming more widely available, backed perhaps on denim, flannel or gaberdine, particularly for children's garments.

Goatskins

These are smaller than sheepskins, and have a very fine, firm texture. Goat suède is durable and hard-wearing. The main use is for shoes, but kidskin is also important for clothing and gloves. Glacé, a term originally describing friction-polished kid, is used also for alum-dressed leathers in gloving weights.

Pigskin

This has a character all its own. The pattern of the bristle holes can be imitated, but not the silky and wrinkled surface that is its particular attraction. A skin is usually about 10 square feet in area.

Pigskin can be finished on the grain or the suède side; or else the grain may be lightly abraded to give a matt finish. It tends to be firmer and thicker (0.7 to 0.9 mm) than the skins of sheep, and presents difficulties in tanning and finishing. Its main use is for accessories such as gloves and for tailored garments, but it can also be produced in a thinner, almost 'dress' weight (0.6 mm), which gives a most beautiful soft drape.

Being scarcer than the other garment leathers, pigskin may therefore be more expensive. The reason is that all hides and skins are by-products; nobody rears an animal for its hide alone, so the supply depends on the amount of meat, milk or wool produced. In fact, fellmongers used to travel round the countryside, collecting raw skins discarded after the fleeces had been removed. The case of pork presents a nice dilemma: while we buy our bacon with the rind on, and prefer our Sunday joint with crackling, there will continue to be a shortage of pigskin.

Deerskin

This, too, has its own characteristic handle. It is softer than pigskin, and has a distinctive cloth-like feel. It comes, as one would expect, from Scotland and looks its best, usually suèded, made up into outdoor styles. It is becoming scarce.

Antelope and gazelle

These give beautifully fine, silky suèdes for the most elegant garments or for trimming. Antelope can also be frized on the grain side, a process that leaves a suède-like finish.

Reptile skins

These have been used mostly for shoe uppers, bags and leather goods. Lizard is still so used, being very tough. Crocodile, now scarce, is almost indestructible. However, snake skins, particularly whip-snake, are now being soft-dressed, which makes them pliable enough for clothing, though because of their narrowness they are usually seen as strips between panels of suède or fur. They are effective and eye-catching in small areas, as a contrast to suède; and of course as belts and edge-trims. Snake is not a strong skin and is always mounted on a staying fabric.

Skins of birds

These are chiefly valued for their distinctive surface texture. Examples are ostrich and emu, both of which can be used for handbags, often in combination with grain leather or suède.

Synthetic leathers

These plastic-coated materials are being improved continually in appearance and drape. They are not an alternative to leather, but complementary to it at the lower end of the market.

The first of the synthetics was Vinyl (Polyvinyl-chloride) which has a shiny surface and a firm, rather unsympathetic handle. It is usually in the form of a thick plastic film on a woven fabric backing, with or without an intervening layer of foam.

The Polyurethane synthetics have a much softer character, spongy and convincingly leather-like, and with better qualities of drape. They may be backed by woven or knitted fabrics.

There are also the mock suèdes. The cheaper ones, made of thick fabric flocked on one side, or woven with a pile, are useful for boys' jackets etc., but have little fashion appeal. However, the best kind is, like felt, homogeneous throughout its thickness; but it has great strength and dimensional stability, and handles beautifully. It is almost indistinguishable from real suède; so is its price. However, since it is bought from the roll, there is less waste in making up.

Ciré fabrics may also be made to resemble leather. In fact, they are simply woven fabrics with their surface polished to a high gloss.

THE STRUCTURE OF LEATHER

Because leather was once the skin of an animal, its structure varies according to the part of the body it originally covered, and according to the growth of the hair or wool.

Hides and skins are thickest down the butt, or centre of the back, where there is usually a heavier ridge of hair. The skin of the belly is thinner, supple and stretchable. The four small areas between the belly and the inside of the legs, known as the *axillae*, have skin of quite a different texture – thin, papery, with fewer hair cells and of lower tensile strength than the rest of the skin. It is used with caution, and in inconspicuous positions, in the manufacture of garments.

The structure of leather is not uniform throughout its thickness. It is composed of minutely fine collagen fibrils, making up fibres which in turn are collected together in bundles. These fibre bundles are interwoven with each other in a three-dimensional pattern through the thickness of the hide. They give leather its elastic but stable structure, and its flexibility. The spaces between the fibre bundles provide its unique, spongy texture, and its capacity to absorb and give off moisture, and to insulate the body with trapped air. As a result leather is comfortable to wear in hot, cold, damp or dry conditions.

The bundles of fibres become finer near the grain surface, which they meet at a blunt angle over most of the skin. This contributes to the fine, tight surface pattern, and characteristic creases, which have such aesthetic appeal. On the belly, however, the fibre bundles lie at a much more acute angle to the surface, resulting on the grain side in a looser texture, and on the flesh side in a longer nap and a less fine suède.

The fibre bundles, interwoven most firmly in the middle of the section through the hide, tend nearer the flesh side to run horizontally, so that the underside of the leather is less frequently attached to the flesh of the animal. Leather, in fact, has a natural termination on the flesh side. Think how easily a rabbit or chicken skin will peel off the carcass, and one can see the parallel with leather. *(Figure 3)*

17

Section through a hide. The hair follicles lie diagonally
in the grain layer. The corium below shows the
interweaving of the fibre bundles. (Magnified x33).

In the axillae, the grain pattern is quite different, almost scaly in appearance, with the creases forming a much coarser pattern, and on the reverse, a very shaggy nap. *(Figure 4)*

The main thickness of leather, from the hair roots inwards, is known as the *corium*. In cattle hides, this may be as much as five-sixths of the total; in sheep, as little as half. In hides, the horizontal division into grain and flesh splits is made just below the roots of the hair, so that the hair cells come into the grain split, along with a small amount of corium. The reason for the weakness of middle splits is that they have neither the fine, tight texture, nor the limiting horizontal weave of the outer splits. In pigskin, the bristle holes extend right through the corium, and appear in the same pattern on the flesh side.

The tiny creases which give leather its character and appeal are known as the break of the leather. They are best seen by bending and folding it. The fineness of the break depends on how firmly the grain is attached to its underlying corium. Where there are many sweat glands and fat cells at the hair roots, which are dried out and emptied during tanning, discontinuity may arise between the grain layer and the corium, showing on the surface as a more coarsely-creased pattern. If this is very pronounced, it is regarded as a fault, and known as looseness.

figure 4

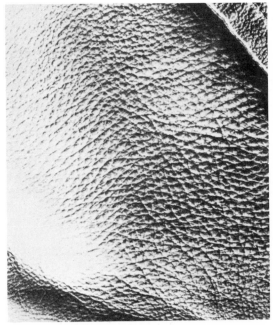 

The coarse grain pattern and shaggy nap of axillae leather.

PROCESSING CLOTHING LEATHERS

There can be few greater contrasts than that between the raw, filthy, matted, stinking sheepskins that enter a tannery, and the beautifully coloured, soft, sweet-smelling leathers that leave it. Only its sheer strength makes it possible for the leather fibre structure to withstand all the mechanical, chemical and heat processes needed to make the transformation.

Much leather is produced in tropical countries, with lower labour costs. This is vegetable-tanned, as it has been for centuries, resulting in brownish, stiff, firm-textured leathers, which are not light-fast. They are used mainly for shoe soles, industrial belting, handbags and luggage, but not for fashion.

Curing

In this country, most skins used for clothing arrive at the tannery in their raw state, often from abroad, where they will have been dry- or wet-salted to kill bacteria. This curing keeps them temporarily from putrefaction. First, therefore, the skins are soaked in an alkaline solution with detergents to get rid of the salt. They are then sprayed on the flesh side with a depilatory to dissolve the keratin which holds the hair in its roots. The hair can then be scraped away from the grain side. The skins are put in a bath of slaked lime or caustic soda, for one or two days, to swell and soften them, to dissolve the proteins out of their fibres, and to open up their structure. This is following by *bating*, a process where enzymes are used to neutralize the alkalinity of the skins, to break up muscle fibre and increase porosity. This is the process that determines the final character and elasticity of the skin; it can be given different qualities of drape, handle and softness, either for clothing or shoe leather.

The skins are then *pickled* in acid and salt, at which stage they can be safely preserved for up to two years, if need be, before tanning. There is thus a reserve of skins ready for tanning and dyeing as needed.

Tanning

The process begins by fleshing, to remove mechanically any loose fibres. The skins are then de-greased, and their smell is distinctly improved. There follows washing in a brine solution, and then tanning.

The tanning agents may be vegetable, synthetic vegetable, or mineral, or any combination of these. But modern clothing leathers have been made possible by the evolution of the mineral chrome-tanning process. At the end of the last century, the demand was growing for leather that was water-resistant, heat-resistant and capable of being coloured with the new synthetic dyestuffs. The first chrome leathers were all these – they were actually resistant to boiling water – but they were also extremely hard. It was later discovered that they could be given softness and drape by treating them with soaps and oils. Some chrome-tanned leathers are now washable, and all are dry-cleanable. So chrome-tanning has brought about a major change in the properties of leather. It is also faster and cheaper than vegetable tanning, taking hours as against months. All this explains why it is now used for almost all clothing leathers and shoe uppers manufactured in this country.

Imported vegetable-tanned skins of hair-sheep are often re-tanned with chrome, and are known as semi-chrome leathers. Chrome-tanned skins may themselves be re-tanned subsequently with aluminium or zirconium salts to improve their dyeing and handling properties; or with glutaraldehyde, which renders leather resistant to sweat.

Tanning is carried out in huge revolving drums, from which the skins emerge an unmistakeable bluish-white colour. They are then neutralized in a solution of sodium bicarbonate, to remove the acidic salts formed during tanning; and afterwards treated in a bath of fat liquor (containing whale, fish or vegetable oil) to restore their suppleness. Next, they are set out between rollers, extended by toggles on wire mesh frames to give a stretched, smooth surface, dried slowly, and cooled back. Finally, they are staked – worked mechanically or by hand over a blunt, semi-circular metal edge to soften them. At this stage, as mordant or crust leather, they can be kept undyed until needed.

Dyeing

The tanned skins are first sorted to give dye-lots matched for quality, texture and thickness; only those free of natural dark markings are selected for dyeing to pale colours. The skins are prepared for dyeing by shaving or buffing to bring them to an even thickness. The fine, one-way nap of suède is produced now by abrading with high-speed carborundum wheels.

Dyeing is in wooden drums, containing up to 500 skins, and using aniline dyes. Oils are added to the dye drum – to lubricate the leather – and metallic soaps or fluorocarbons may be included, or applied after dyeing, to improve water resistance and shower-proofing. Some nappas and suèdes may not be dyed in drum, but instead brush-dyed on one surface only; this is usual for dark-coloured gloving leathers, leaving a natural-coloured inside to the glove, and avoiding dark crockings – loose particles of fibre – on the hand.

The skins are again set out, dried under controlled conditions of temperature and humidity, and cooled back. For a suède finish, that side is buffed up and brushed. For grain leathers, a further process of pigmenting may be needed – spraying with an acrylic resin coating to level up the colour. This is followed by a final staking and then polishing on felt rollers. Lastly, a top-coat of nitro-cellulose gives a spongeable surface for easy care. Polyurethane or 'wet-look' finishes, if used, are applied at this stage: there is still a problem of cracking and peeling with this finish. Real leather coated in this way is not to be confused with the polyurethane 'leathers', which are backed on fabric.

Measuring and grading

The last processes are measuring by machine – in square feet – the total area of each skin, and grading according to any faults. No two skins are identical. They may have small flay-marks, snags, scars from injections or ticks which make harder or lighter patches of leather; areas of looseness; or vein markings. If these faults are extensive, or preclude the cutting of a large perfect panel from the skin, it will be down-graded and its price accordingly affected.

When one realizes how many processes, some of them using highly-skilled hand labour, are needed to produce fine leather, it no longer seems expensive. One is astonished that it can be manufactured so economically.

THE PROCESSING OF WOOLSKINS

Woolskins include both shearlings, made from the skins of adult sheep, and lambskins with softer, shorter and curlier wool. The best skins for clothing are either domestic, or from New Zealand. Australian skins are valued for their curly wool, often made up on the outside of garments. Some merino breeds, ideal for beaver lamb or for rugs, are not satisfactory as shearlings. Their wool is so thick and heavy that discontinuity can occur at the hair roots, showing on the suède side as a series of folds or ridges running out from the backbone, and known as ribbiness, really an extreme case of looseness. *(Figure 5)*

Ridges on the suède side of a merino skin, a fault known as ribbiness.

The first process is to remove grass, mud and foreign bodies from the wool with a de-burring machine. The skins are then scoured with paddles in soda and detergent. Fleshing follows, and the skins are pickled in acid and salt, as for grain leathers.

Chrome-tannage is usual, in great wooden vats, in which the skins and liquor are kept moving by wooden paddle-wheels of a size that might have driven a ship. (Although the use of so much wooden machinery seems at first sight surprising, in fact it is far more efficient than metal in its resistance to chemical action, its gentleness to the skins, and its ease of maintenance and replacement.) Tanning is followed by spin-drying, and stretching out on metal frames for further drying. Woolskins have to be seasoned, so after drying they are lightly sprayed

figure 5

with water, and kept damp. After that, they are tumbled in revolving cages to soften them, flexed on staking machines, and given a final scraping to clean off any remaining flesh. They are de-greased in benzene. At this stage, skins to be used for beaver lamb are ironed with formaldehyde to straighten and brighten the wool.

The dyeing of woolskins is complicated by the requirements of both the wool and the skin. Dyes for wool need to be fast to heat and ironing. Suède dyes must be fast to light, abrasion and rain, but must not affect the white wool; resist-dyeing is used, which colours the skin but leaves the wool unaffected.

The suède surface is now raised by wheeling, and stoned for a finer nap. Lastly, the wool is combed, clipped and finish-ironed. In all, the woolskins pass through about 40 processes.

BUYING LEATHER

Problems

Choosing – indeed obtaining – the right kind of leather is perhaps the most awkward problem the amateur has to solve. As a sizeable outlay of money may be involved, you cannot afford to buy leather that is unsuitable for the garment you have in mind, or indeed that is worthless for any garment. The all-important point is to know what you are buying – its animal origin, thickness, handle, kind of tanning and dye-fastness. This means dealing with a supplier who can guarantee what he is selling. It is most unwise to buy skins that cannot be dry-cleaned. To be sure they are dry-cleanable, one must know that they have been chrome-tanned. A simple test for this is to burn a scrap of the leather. If it is chrome-tanned, it will leave a bright green ash. This still gives no clue, though, as to whether the skin is washable, or dye-fast.

Leathers sold by saddlers for bags and linings are not suitable for making up into garments; neither are the skin skivers, so delicately thin and beautifully coloured, which are prepared for book-binding – they are vegetable-tanned, and will not wash, dry-clean or keep their shape. One might try a small piece for a belt, though, if backed by fabric or suède.

A good supplier will be able to describe exactly what he is selling, how it is tanned and whether it is washable, dry-cleanable and dye-fast. Here, a further problem arises. Many reliable suppliers do not deal in small quantities, as the cost of handling orders for individual garments far outweighs the return. However, firms are sometimes willing to sell a few skins, from their warehouses for spot cash, so long as no expensive paper-work is involved. It is well worth-while seeking out any tanneries or leather merchants in your area, and trying your luck.

There are many advantages in seeing the skins before you buy. It is easier to judge substance and handle from a whole skin, than from a sample a few inches square. The important points are that the leather should be of the right weight and softness for the garment you plan to make, and for the limitations of your machine. There is a vast range of leathers from the thickest of bovine splits, through all the weights of domestic and Cape nappas and shirt suèdes, to the finest of gloving glacés and suèdes. If you cannot get exactly what you want, it is better to redesign the garment than to use a leather unsuitable for your pattern. It cannot be stressed too strongly that, until you are experienced, it is better to stick to the thinner and more supple leathers, or to chamois.

Another advantage of seeing before buying, is that you can consider lower-grade skins. Their grading has nothing to do with tanning or the general quality of the leather; only with the number and position of faults. You may find such faults as looseness, vein marks, snags or uneven dye patches. Unless you need very large panels, you may well find it more economical to buy low-grade skins, and allow extra leather, say 20 per cent, for wastage. As low-grade skins may be less than half the price of the top grade, the saving could be considerable.

What is essential is that you should buy all your skins at the same time, and be sure you have enough, as it may not be possible to match exactly from another batch. Matching is not only for colour, but also for weight, grain texture and, in the case of shearlings, for density and character of the wool.

At the end of the book is a list of first-class suppliers of all kinds of leather and fittings, who are also willing to deal with small orders by post.

The Quantities

Hides are bought whole, or by the side, butt or belly. They are priced per square foot. The belly is cheaper and far easier to handle, not being as thick as butt leather. Skins are bought whole, also priced per square foot. *(Figure 6)*

The difficulty is in knowing the quantity to buy. Because of the shape of skins, one must expect a high percentage of waste. Even professional cutters expect to lose up to 40 per cent of the total skin area in edges, faults and uncuttable shapes. More than this in shearlings. Compare this to the very much smaller percentage of waste when working with fabric.

The easiest method is to look up the quantity of fabric needed by your pattern, and reduce this to square feet (9 sq. ft to the yard, 36 in. wide; 13.5 sq. ft to the yard, 54 in. wide). We must still work in yards and feet, because leather is still sold by the square foot. To this number, add one-fifth (or two-fifths, if working with low-grade skins) to allow for wastage. You will now have the number of square feet needed. If ordering by post, give this number, and the supplier will send the right quantity of skins. If you can see the skins before buying, each will be marked with its area – usually about 6 square feet – so you can buy accordingly. If in doubt, always be generous. There are so many uses for small quantities of surplus leather, from bags and belts to trimming on fabric garments.

Suppose, for example, that your garment needs 2 yards of 54-in. wide fabric. This works out at 27 square feet. Add one-fifth, say 6 square feet, and the total you will need is 33 square feet, representing five or six skins, according to size. If working with low-grade skins, then allow one extra skin, about 6 square feet. Or use the table opposite as a very rough guide.

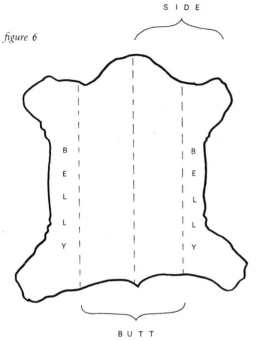

SIDE

figure 6

BUTT

	Skins needed
Skirts, 60 cm (24 in.)–66 cm (26 in.) long	3
Shirts	4
Short-sleeved blouses	3
Men's shirts	5
Long-sleeved jackets, 63 cm (25 in.) long	4 or 5
Three-quarter length coats, 84 cm (33 in.) long	6
Full length coats, 112 cm (44 in.) long	6 or 7
Men's coats	7 or 8
Short boleros	1½
Waistcoats	2
Long waistcoats or jerkins	3
Ties	1
Belts	1
Trousers	6
Handbags	1

BUYING LEATHER GARMENTS

Even when one can deal successfully with the thinner leathers, one would not attempt to compete with the specialist manufacturers in tackling tailored, full-length garments in shearling or the heavier leathers. So a few points to watch for when buying garments may be useful.

The most important decision is whether to buy, for instance, a more expensive coat with the label and guarantee of a well-known manufacturer, or whether to go down the road and buy a similar-looking coat at half the price, without either. The difficulty lies in discovering whether the two garments really are of similar quality.

First-class manufacturers take a great deal of trouble to ensure that the skins they use are top-grade and of suitable weight. Skins are matched for colour, surface texture and drape, and weak or loose parts are not used. The quality of the lining, buttons, etc., will match the quality of the garment. The whole process of manufacture is carefully controlled, and any work or material that is less than perfect will down-grade the garment.

The dry-cleaning guarantee is of great importance. It ensures that a garment that is dirty but in good condition will look as new after cleaning. The label of a good manufacturer in itself means that any fault appearing in the garment will be remedied, or in extreme cases that the garment may even be replaced. In effect, the price charged in the first place covers a number of services, as well as being an assurance of quality.

If, however, one is considering a much cheaper, non-branded garment, one might in some cases find a bargain. 'Seconds' from a good manufacturer may have only small faults; if they can be identified, one may be willing to accept them for the sake of the difference in price. Sometimes there may be a few garments at the end of a run, in odd sizes and at lower prices. However, one should be extremely careful to watch for such points as these:

Does the garment hang well? Are the pitch and drape satisfactory?

Is the leather supple?

Is there plenty of substance in the leather across the back? Are the collar and facings close and tight in texture?

Are there any patches of looseness that may become more pronounced in wear?

Are the right and left sides well matched for texture, colour and thickness of skin? This is a frequent cause of down-grading.

Is the quality of the lining satisfactory? This is one of the commonest faults in cheap garments, and re-lining is a tedious operation. See page 107.

Are the buttons secured by small backing buttons? Are the buttonholes well made? Are there backing buttons inside the corners of any pockets that will take much wear?

Is any zip firmly set in, particularly the tape ends at the opening?

Is the size of the garment right? Extra ease is needed in leather garments; shearlings need to be as much as 15 to 18 cm (6 in. to 7 in.) bigger than your hip measurement. There should be no pull on the buttons.

Are the sleeves wide enough? A too-tight sleeve will soon cause strain at the armhole.

In shearlings, does the wool run downwards, in the body and in the sleeves? On some cheaper garments manufacturers may economize by neglecting this point; but sleeves of sweaters or shirts will ride up uncomfortably inside shearling sleeves that are cut the wrong way of the wool.

Are bindings or edge finishes well stitched, particularly at the ends?

If the answers to all or most of these questions are satisfactory, you are likely to have found a coat by a good manufacturer, perhaps one of a batch made to keep production going during a slack period. In that case, you will have a bargain. But perhaps your sharpened eye will have found too many faults to think that the cheaper garment is really similar to the branded one.

As to the more exotic garments imported from tropical countries, or especially those bought in their country of origin, one should be very careful indeed. White shaggy sheepskins may well be salt-alum tawed, which means that they are little more than rough-cured, and will have no resistance to heat or dampness. A test – if you can bring yourself to do it – is to touch the suède surface with your tongue. A salty taste indicates this type of dressing.

Other problems with imperfectly tanned sheepskins, whether clothing or rugs, include the possibility, admittedly remote, of tick eggs hatching out in the fleece, owing to the warmth of the body. Less uncommon may be an increasingly unpleasant smell, due to the putrefaction of incompletely or unevenly tanned leather. It is a safeguard to buy this kind of garment from a good shop or store, rather than from a market. You will then have the protection of the buyer's knowledge.

Patterns
for Leather

DESIGNING FOR LEATHER

Almost all the clothing leathers now used in this country come from sheep. Their skins average only 5 to 7 square feet, and the best parts are down the centre back and sides of the animal. So patterns for leather garments should have smaller, narrower panels, and more seaming. This not only allows scope for more interesting design; but also gives support to the leather, as the extra seams help to strengthen it, and prevent it from stretching in wear. Examples of good styling would be the use of yokes, centre back and waist seams, and inset bands at waist and cuff. Sleeves are usually cut in two parts, a top and an under-sleeve, as in a man's suit, both for economical cutting and also to make the sleeve hang better. Trousers must have a seam at knee level.

The kind of garment you want will determine, first of all, the weight and substance of the skins needed, and then the kind of pattern to suit the skins.

For straight-cut, functional garments

Suitable leathers would be bovine nappa, suède split, or the firmer sheep nappas. You would plan the simple seaming and clean lines of a classic shape, with design detail confined to top-stitching or decorative edge treatments. Sleeveless garments or panelled skirts are easy to make in this weight of leather. Trousers might be too stiff and hot. *(Figure 1)*

The commercial patterns made especially for leather are usually designed for these heavier qualities. Their sleeve-heads are less full than in patterns designed for fabric, and not cut so deep. The reason is that the heavier leathers will not accept much ease, so the sleeve must be very little wider than the armhole. Ordinary patterns may therefore have to be adapted by taking out some of the width and height at the sleeve-head. *(Figure 2)*

In firm leathers, darts are difficult to flatten. It is usually better to make a dart into a seam; this will also help to save leather, by using narrower panels. *(Figure 3)*

figure 1

Collars in this weight of leather are not easy to tackle, so in your first garment it is best to plan for a single-thickness collar rather than a faced one. *(Figure 4)*

For softer, more feminine styles

Choose one of the thinner nappas, or a shirt suède, or indeed chamois. Because it is easy to handle, and much cheaper than the dyed and more highly finished leathers, chamois would be an ideal choice for your first leather garment. Any of these weights would make up into beautifully soft styles. You would be able to use gathers into yokes or cuffs, even tucks, frills, flared peplums, godets and pleats. You could bind the edges, or use shaped and turned facings to give a scalloped finish. There is no end to the design possibilities for these fine and supple skins. *(Figure 5)*

PREPARING THE PATTERN

When you have chosen a pattern, and made sure that it is suitable for the type of garment, and the type of leather you have in mind, then you must begin by adapting the pattern to the leather.

Leather does need a little extra ease round the body. In a fabric garment, you would expect the bust and hip measurements of the garment to be about 5 cm (2 in.) bigger than your own body measurement. In leather, they should be 7 to 10 cm (3 in. to 4 in.) bigger, depending on the substance and handle of the leather. If you are using a shearling sheepskin, then you should allow as much as 15 to 18 cm (6 in. to 7 in.) extra for an easy fit. Sleeves should be 1 to 2.5 cm ($\frac{1}{2}$ in. to 1 in.) longer than fabric sleeves would be, and, if close-fitting, should be 2.5 cm wider. Trousers need to be 5 cm (2 in.) longer in the leg. This may seem a great deal of extra length, but it is necessary because leather naturally forms creases that settle into your own shape, especially at elbow and knee, and this takes up length from the garment. Check that all your pattern pieces will be wide and long enough.

Where you decide to have extra seams, for instance at yoke or waist, cut across and separate the pattern pieces. Pencil in balance marks (notches), if you need them on long seams. If you are putting in a yoke, with gathers, you will need to widen the lower pattern piece by inserting a strip of paper, and then adding balance marks at each end of the alteration. *(Figure 6)*

Now consider the types of seam you will use. With leather, it is seldom that the same kind would be appropriate right through the whole garment. Some seams should be treated as important decorative features, often top-stitched. Others, such as centre back and underarm seams, are better if they are inconspicuous. Because leather does not fray, turnings can in any case be narrower than on cloth; but on some kinds of seam one or both edges may need no turning at all. So look at the various seams shown on page 43, and decide *at this stage* which kinds you will use. Check the exact turnings needed for each edge, and mark them on your pattern in place of the usual 1.5 cm ($\frac{5}{8}$ in.) allowance. Add also the turnings for any of the *new* seams you have put in.

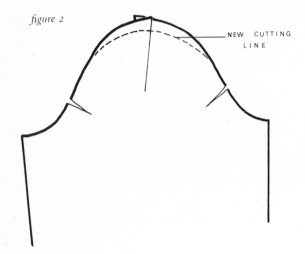

figure 2

NEW CUTTING
LINE

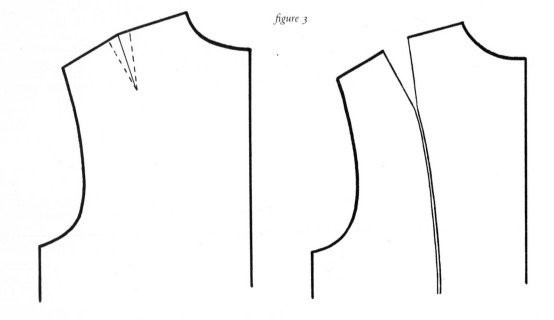

figure 3

Hems on leather garments should be not less than 1.5 cm ($\frac{5}{8}$ in.) nor more than 4 cm ($1\frac{1}{2}$ in.) deep. The stiffer the leather, the deeper the hem. Mark your new hem turnings, too, on the pattern.

You will now have an altered pattern, with exactly the right fit and the right seam and hem allowances, saving you a surprising amount of leather – or rather, making it possible to place your pattern pieces more easily on the better parts of the skins. Even so, it is not safe to cut out the leather yet. Because seams on leather cannot be taken out and altered, you cannot afford any mistakes in fitting. A little patience now can mean the difference between success and an expensive failure.

FITTING

The only sure way to avoid mistakes is to make up a cloth model of the garment first, which itself can become the pattern from which you cut the leather. The model can be made in calico or canvas – or, to save cost, it can equally well be made from pieces of old sheet. These are quite firm enough to give you the idea of the final shape of the garment; they are taken apart after fitting to be used as the pattern. Old sheets are assets never to be thrown out, if you plan to make leather or suède garments.

Begin by cutting out *all* the pattern pieces in the sheeting. Include all facings, belt linings, etc. Cut patterns for both right and left sides, and cut a whole piece (such as the whole width of a back yoke) where the pattern would normally be placed to a fold. This is essential, because leather can *never* be cut in double thickness. It is wise at this stage to mark the *pairs* of pieces, so that you will have, for instance, a *right front* and a *left front*. Mark the patterns with ball-point or felt-tip on their right sides. When you lay them out on the leather, you will know that if the writing is uppermost you will have true pairs.

It is worth taking these seemingly endless precautions at this early stage, because it is almost unbelievably easy to cut two pieces for the same side of the body – two left sleeves, for instance – and there may well not be enough leather left over to cut a replacement.

Transfer the usual dressmaker's markings to the cloth pattern. Particularly important are buttonholes, pocket markings, and the points where seams cross, to give a really accurate outline.

Balance marks are not cut outwards as in ordinary dressmaking. A tailor's chalk or pencil mark at the edge of the seam allowance is better: then, for instance, the straight edge of two pattern pieces can be laid side by side on the leather, with only a single cutting line between them. Use every device to avoid wasting leather.

Cut out and tack up the cloth model, using the exact seam allowances. Try it on and pin together any openings. These are some fitting points to watch for:

The fit of the shoulders. It is easy at this stage to take in the centre back of the neckline for a better fit – quite impossible after cutting out.

The armhole fit. If your shoulders are square, the shoulder seam may need to be let out at its armhole end; if you have sloping shoulders, it may need taking in.

The sleeve. Check the length of the sleeve. Does it hang smoothly, without drag behind or in front of the shoulder seam? Is it wide enough?

The waistline must coincide with yours. There is almost certain to be a waist seam, except in the simplest jerkin patterns. If in doubt, tie a piece of string round your waist, over the fabric model, to see what alteration is needed.

Fastenings. Are the buttonholes or other fastenings at the right height for your figure? One buttonhole should be at the waistline, unless you plan to have a belt.

Pockets. Are their proportions right, and their placing flattering to you? It is worth while experimenting with different pocket shapes, sizes and positions.

The length of the garment should be checked; an unwanted inch can waste a great deal of leather.

When you are quite sure of the fit, the cloth model is taken to pieces, altered where necessary, and used as the final pattern for cutting out the leather.

CUTTING OUT

The 'grain' of leather runs from the neck down the backbone to the tail. There is less stretch in this direction, and the fibres are more firmly interwoven. The surface pattern of the skin may also show a direction, which you must take into account when matching opposite sides of the garment. In suèdes, there is a nap down the skin which, like velvet, shows quite a different shade when seen from the opposite direction. The main pieces should be cut *with the nap*, their tops being placed towards the neck end of the skin. Some pigskin suèdes, though, can be used in any direction.

No two skins are exactly alike. They may have small faults – flay-marks, snags, scratches or discoloured areas – even holes near the edges. The skin of the neck, and down the first few inches of the backbone, may be thicker and less smooth than the rest. This can be specially noticeable as a colour-shading on suèdes. The skin of the axillae is thinner, more stretchable and weaker than the rest. It is not suitable for garments, so save it for patchwork. The belly is softer and more stretchable than the back, and it may dye to a slightly darker shade.

The whole skill of cutting leather is to make the most of these different qualities, and to waste as little as possible of the skins. The best and firmest parts must be used for the largest and most important sections of the garment. Left and right sides must match in texture and colour shading. The thinner parts of the skins make up those sections which either need less strength, or show less in wear. Here are some important points:

The two main foreparts should be cut from the same skin, using your best one. It should be fine-grained, even and firm. There should not, of course, be any faults. The skin should be strong enough for buttonholes, with all the strain they are expected to carry, and perhaps for pocket welts too. Place the two pattern pieces side by side, with their underarm edges at the sides of the skin, where it is most flexible, and the centre fronts together at the middle of the skin where it is firmer. *(Figure 7)*

The back should be cut from a very firm skin. It can be heavier than the others, as it has to take the strain across the back of the shoulders. If there are faults, they matter less at the back of the garment.

Sleeves should be cut from matching skins. Softer, less firm leather is better for sleeves, so that they more easily mould to shoulder and elbow movements. In a pattern with two-part sleeves, cut the top sleeves from a firmer part of the skin (to match the texture of the armholes), and the under-sleeves from the softer, flanky areas nearer the edges. *(Figure 8)*

The top-collar and revers will be the most noticeable part of the garment, so they should be cut from perfect sections of matching, fine-textured leather. A close grain and flexible drape are more important than strength here. The pieces may be cut in any direction of the grain, lengthwise or across.

Facings should be firm, but not as heavy as the leather edge they are facing. If you will be using iron-on interfacing, for instance inside cuffs, then the facings themselves can be in a looser, more flexible leather, such as from the belly edges. Front facings may be seamed below the break of the revers, taking care to avoid buttonhole placings.

Pocket welts, cuffs and waistbands must be cut from very firm sections of leather.

Begin by laying out all your skins, right side up, and with the neck ends all pointing one way. Perhaps the best place for this is on a bed. Look very carefully for faults, and mark them with ordinary blackboard chalk. Tailor's chalk can be difficult to remove, and you may in the end have to use one of these faulty areas for an inside facing or pocket lining.

Lay the fabric pattern pieces on the right side of the leather. Beginning with the largest and most important pieces, lay them out in pairs on the most suitable skins. Make sure again that you *do* have a left and right of each piece, or you may find yourself with one panel reversed. One great advantage of working in leather is that *you need not follow the grain*. Even main pieces, which will have to take a good deal of wear, may be laid at quite an angle to the true grain. It is wise if possible to place the corresponding left and right pieces at more or less the same angle to the grain, but the main consideration is the stretch and feel of the skins. It would not do, for instance, to cut a left piece on grain down the firm, middle part of a skin, and its matching right piece off grain on a thin, flanky section; but this is just common sense. The stretch of the leather should be *round the body*, as it was on the animal, not up and down. *(Figure 9)*

When the main pieces have been placed, lay out the smaller or less conspicuous ones, filling in every inch of useful leather. When you are quite sure of the placing of *all* the pieces, move one skin at a time to the cutting-out table. Smooth out and hold the cloth patterns in place with a few small pieces of Sellotape. Do *not* be tempted to pin round the edges as this would only distort the shape of the skin, and the pieces might not cut out evenly.

Cut out with sharp, long-bladed dressmaking shears, using smooth, long strokes and holding the pattern down with the flat of your other hand. A cloth pattern clings well to the leather, and is far easier to manage than a flimsy paper pattern. It is seldom that a modern, clothing-weight leather is too thick for shears. A scalpel or leather-knife is *not* necessary and unless you are expert it is difficult to control precisely – apart from the inevitable damage to the cutting-out surface.

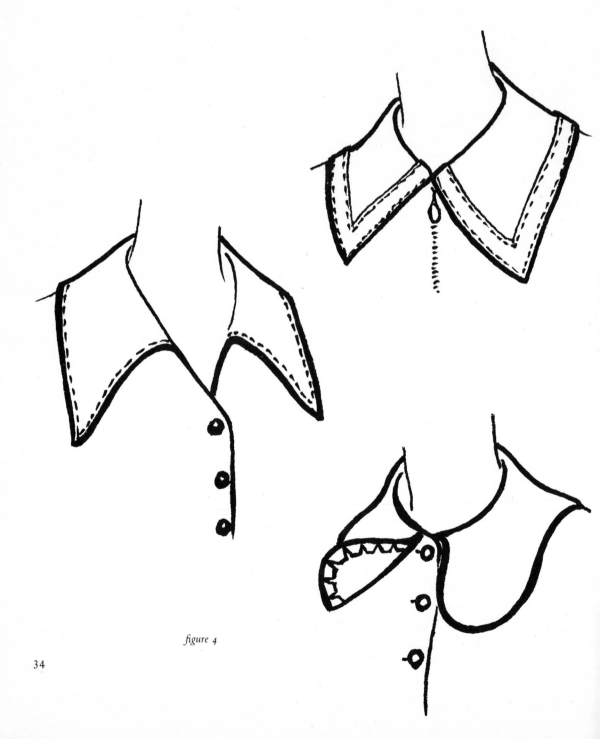

figure 4

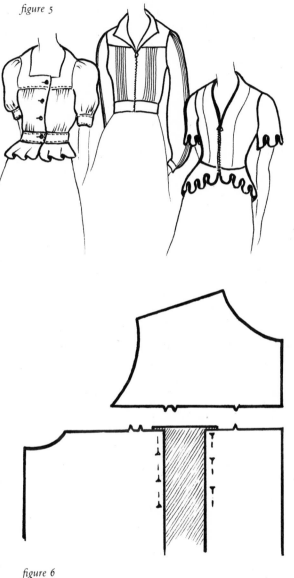

figure 5

figure 6

MARKING

On grain leather and suède, you cannot use the normal dressmaker's marking aids such as tailor's tacks or tracing wheel. Needle and pin marks are permanent, and show up clearly even on napped suèdes, while the spikes of a tracing wheel could also leave marks. So all marking on garment pieces should be:

On the *right* side, using only ordinary blackboard chalk, which will brush off, or better,

On the *wrong* side, using tailor's chalk or pencil, neither of which will come off easily, but which do not matter on that side. One advantage of leathers is that, however thin they are, nothing marked on the wrong side will show through. Another method is:

On the *wrong* side, marking with pencil through dressmaker's carbon paper. But never try to mark through two thicknesses of leather as you would with cloth; leather is too thick for this to be successful.

Transfer all the markings you made on the pattern, to the leather. Make sure that each side is marked at exactly the same points, checking particularly the matching of pocket placings.

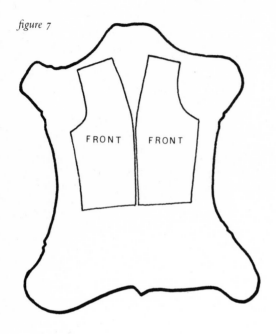

figure 7

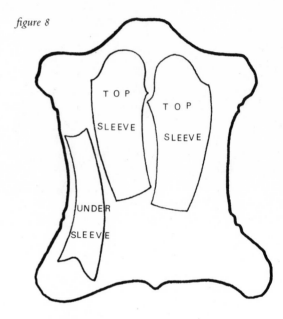

figure 8

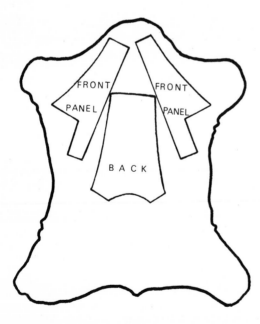

figure 9

Sewing Leather

The structure and thickness of leather make many of the usual dressmaking processes either inappropriate or simply unworkable. It is difficult for an experienced dressmaker to put aside almost all she knows about sewing fabrics, and begin again from the beginning; but quite different techniques are needed to control the material, particularly during the early stages of garment construction. One should cultivate the habit of questioning every single step: processes which are almost second nature in the sewing of fabric may be disastrous in leather.

Before embarking on the garment itself, it is helpful to get used to the leather by practising on small scraps until one has the 'feel' of how it will work. Leather is a very sympathetic material and the actual working of it shows, better than written instructions, how it needs to be handled.

PRESSING

The tanning of chrome leather allows it to withstand heat. Pressing is just as necessary for leather as for fabric – to remove creases, settle down seam turnings, and attach fusible interfacings. But special precautions must be taken:

Do not use steam, or a damp pressing cloth.

Press with a sheet of brown paper between the iron and the leather, and between each thickness of leather. This is especially important under seam edges, to stop a ridge forming on the right side of the leather. Brown paper is better than a pressing cloth, which might leave traces of cotton lint – difficult to remove from suède.

Set the iron at its lowest setting, as for Acrilan or Courtelle. Only if this setting is not enough, should you put it up to the second setting, as for wool; never higher. Remember that an iron may overheat when first switched on. Leave it for a few minutes to allow the thermostat time to cut in.

POUNDING

Pounding is an alternative to pressing, especially useful for small areas such as buttonholes, points of collars or pocket corners. This gentle hammering, or tapping, with a small, smooth weight is a most important and useful technique. It compresses and redistributes the fibre bundles, and so can be used to flatten seams without using heat. It can actually reduce the thickness of the leather. It is factory practice to use a polished steel weight, shaped like a hammer-head, but with a slightly domed surface. A silversmith's planishing hammer has this shape. Otherwise, use an ordinary small hammer, so long as it has a smooth, unpitted face. A little practice on scraps will show how much pounding is needed, and how heavy it should be.

STICKING AND ADHESIVES

After pressing or pounding, seam turnings and hems are held in place with adhesive, either alone, or in preparation for top-stiching. The choice of adhesive is of great importance. Use *only* those that will stand either washing or dry-cleaning.

Copydex

This latex cement is reliable and convenient. It is widely used in factory production. As it does not set for about half a minute, a wrongly-stuck edge can be lifted and re-laid. Any traces left accidentally on the surface of the leather can be rubbed off with a finger when dry, or lifted off with a rolled-up ball of the dried adhesive; but not from the suède side. Copydex is safe for washing, and, as all the glove-weight leathers are now washable, it is perhaps the most useful of the adhesives. In dry-cleaning, it will dissolve completely, so hems will need to be stuck back in place by the cleaner.

Bostik No 1

This is safe for both washing and dry-cleaning. It is therefore better for a lined garment that will need cleaning.

Some other household or hobby adhesives may partially dissolve in dry-cleaning fluids, and melt out over the garment itself during the process, making tacky patches that are impossible to shift. Do not risk a result like the sleeve shown here, ruined after adhesive from the interfacing had re-set. *(Figure 1)*

Three points to check when using adhesives:

Press or pound before sticking, to flatten the seam or hem.

Use as little adhesive as possible, on a small spatula or the blade of a knife. Smooth down the stuck edges with your fingers. If adhesive will not easily hold on a polished leather, abrade its surface lightly with an emery board.

Do not stick the whole turning of a hem. A depth of 1 cm ($\frac{3}{8}$ in.) close to the fold is enough. This will leave the edge free for attaching the lining.

Sleeve ruined after dry-cleaning has caused an
unsuitable adhesive from the interfacing to melt and
re-set.

figure 1

SKIVING

The thickness of leather edges can be reduced by skiving – shaving off part of the leather on the wrong side. Most modern leathers, being thinner and more flexible, should not need skiving. It may also be risky (to the leather as well as to fingers) unless you are skilful with a razor blade.

Practise *first* with a small piece of leather, on a chopping board. Stroke the razor blade, or sharp hobbyknife, away from you, and cut off a slanting slice along the edge of the leather. *(Figure 2)*

Only when you are quite sure that you can control the blade, should you move to the garment itself. Fold the whole of it out of the way, towards you, leaving just the single seam-turning flat on the chopping board. Stroke the knife-blade away from you (and from the garment) in diagonal strokes along the edge of the leather.

The most important use of skiving is to join strips of leather end-to-end, to make trims or strappings. These strips are much easier to control than garment edges. Simply reduce the thickness of the last centimetre ($\frac{3}{8}$ in.) of one strip on the *wrong* side, and the thickness of the next strip on the *right* side, and they are ready to be stuck together and pounded. *(Figure 3)*

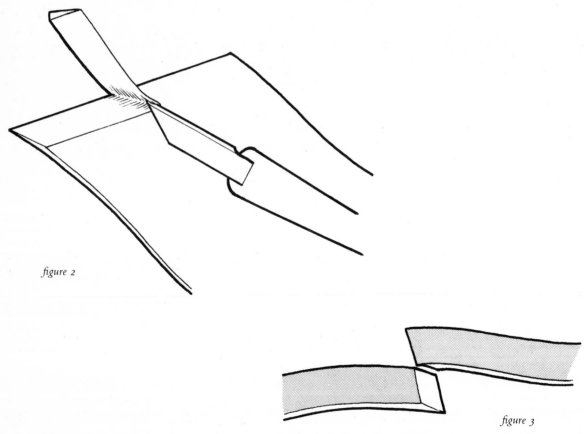

figure 2

figure 3

40

ALTERNATIVES
TO PINNING AND TACKING

Any holes made in leather are permanent. They do not close up again behind the needle, as do holes in woven or knitted fabrics. Machine stitching cannot be unpicked and re-done in a different place, as this will always leave a row of dots, not only ugly but also weakening to the fibre structure. Never pin or tack on leather or suède. It is hard in any case to push pins through. There are better ways to hold garment pieces together before stitching.

For flat seams, or anywhere the right sides of the leather are placed together, use clips to hold the edges. Paper-clips are usually recommended, but they are not easy to pull off as you stitch up to them, without distorting the seam. Hair-clips – the kind with a spring end and two prongs – are much better, and hold the leather firmly enough. Use them at intervals of 10 to 15 cm (4 in. to 6 in.) along the seam. For more substantial garments, use clothes pegs.

For overlaid seams, or anywhere a right side is placed to a wrong side, use Copydex. Just spread it along one edge, lap the other edge over it, and pound or press with your fingers. It makes a perfectly safe bond before top-stitching. This method is also useful for sticking the edges of patch pockets to the garment, otherwise a problem to hold in place for top-stitching.

For setting in zips, or any work that can be held together from the wrong side, use Sellotape or masking tape. This gives a secure basis for stitching and can be torn away afterwards. (*Figure 4.*) Do not use Sellotape on the *right* side, as it may lift off the pigment from grain leather, or the nap from suède. (*Never* let a charity flag-seller put one of her sticky flags on your leather or suède jacket as the mark may not come off until the garment is dry-cleaned.)

For top-stitching collar necklines, you could even use a stapler. So long as the staples are in line with the stitching, the thread will cover their holes. Winkle them out as you sew up to them. See page 60.

MACHINING

Leather is difficult to sew by hand, and in practice machining makes a far better job of it. Ordinary domestic machines will sew any modern clothing leathers. It is not even necessary to have a swing-needle machine; there is much to be said for the old hand machines – not least that they can be worked very slowly and with greater control.

Basic rules for machining leather

Lighten the pressure on the foot of the machine, so that the layers of leather will slip through easily, and will not be marked by the teeth in the needle-plate. Experiment with different pressures, until the leather moves smoothly and the stitch length stays even. If a polished leather, or a Vinyl, does tend to stick, rub a little talcum powder on the needle-plate. This will be quite easy to brush out of the machine, and off the garment. Or use a Teflon foot, if your machine can be fitted with one.

The stitch length must be *at least* 3 mm ($\frac{1}{8}$ in.). Stitches smaller than this weaken the leather dramatically, and may result in tearing when much strain is put on the seam. Needle-punctures 3 mm apart leave 2 mm of leather in between; but if you use only a 2 mm stitch (quite usual on cloth), then the sound leather left between the stitches is reduced 50 per cent to only 1 mm – not enough for a strong seam. You can even set the longest stitch your machine will make, 4 to 5 mm ($\frac{3}{16}$ in.).

You may need to alter the thread tensions, especially when top-stitching with heavier threads. Check the tensions before stitching each seam; leather has a propensity for throwing thread-tensions out of balance.

Stitch *slowly* to keep the stitch-length even. This is the most difficult part of learning to sew leather, particularly where seams cross, making an extra thickness. Practise first on scraps, until you have got the feel of the leather, using the same number of thicknesses as in the garment. Use the slow gear, if your machine has one, as it gives extra power – and remember that, with long stitches, you may travel faster than you expect. Do not pull the leather through the machine, but hold it firmly stretched between your hands and guide it through. If the leather is taut, the machine teeth will keep the stitch even.

As there can be no question of unpicking, you must be quite certain that the first stitching will be in the right place. Use the edge of the presser-foot, or an edge-guide, to ensure that you stitch exactly on the seamline.

Needles

Machine needles made especially for sewing leather are invaluable for the thicker, more substantial leathers, and for all top-stitching. A useful size for most purposes is Metric Size 100 (U.S. Size 16); 90s (14s) are for lighter-weight nappas; and 80s (12s) for the finest suèdes and chamois. The spear-shaped point of these needles gives extra cutting power. The only drawback is that the square holes they make may tear more easily than the perfectly round holes made by ordinary needles, as any engineer will tell you. This need not be a problem so long as the stitch is kept long.

Threads

Cotton threads are not strong enough for leather, and linen thread may be too heavy for your machine. The special threads used in factory production, even if they were available retail, would be unsuitable for feeding into most domestic machines. So use polyester. For flat seams on the lighter leathers, Skanthread or Gütermann's Polyester are suitable. But for hides, for most skins and for all top-stitching, a much bolder effect is obtained with buttonhole-twists such as Skanthread Goliath, Dewhurst's Bold, or Gütermann's Polytwist.

For any hand-sewing, use one of these twists, but first draw the thread over a lump of beeswax to prevent tangling. A thimble is essential for hand-sewing; and a gloving needle, with its triangular point, pierces leather more easily. Hand-sewing along a leather edge can be made much easier by first running the machine, unthreaded, along the stitching line, and then sewing through the needle-holes.

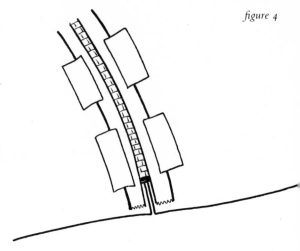

figure 4

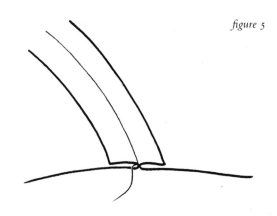

figure 5

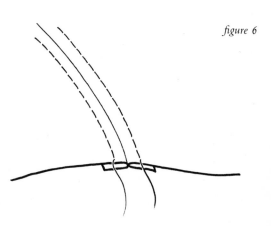

figure 6

SEAMS

Seams take on great importance in leather garments. They are more conspicuous than in cloth, and should be considered as design features to give character to the garment. No edge-neatening is needed on leather, of course, so turnings may be narrower than on fabric.

Flat seam

Good for inconspicuous seams at underarm and shoulder on any thickness of leather. Also for fake leathers or brush-dyed suèdes, where the cut edges should not show. Allow 1.2 cm ($\frac{1}{2}$ in.) turnings. Pound or press, and stick down. *(Figure 5)*

Top-stitched seam

Press or pound open the seam turnings, hold them down with a trace of adhesive, and top-stitch from the right side, using the edge of the presser-foot as a guide to straight stitching. Set the longest possible stitch – often effective with a contrasting coloured buttonhole twist. Allow 1.2 cm ($\frac{1}{2}$ in.) turnings. *(Figure 6)*

Double-stitched seam

Good for yoke seams. Allow a 1.2 cm ($\frac{1}{2}$ in.) turning on one piece, but only 6 mm ($\frac{1}{4}$ in.) on the other. After the first stitching, pound or press the turnings flat, both in the same direction, so that the narrower one is enclosed. Stitch again, on the right side, catching in the wider turning. *(Figure 7)*

Overlaid seam

Similar to the last seam, except that there is only one row of stitching. This seam is suitable for the finer leathers. Fold over and stick down the seam turning on the overlap. Move this folded edge into place on the underlap (holding with Sellotape on the wrong side) and stitch. Allow 1.2 cm turnings. *(Figure 8)*

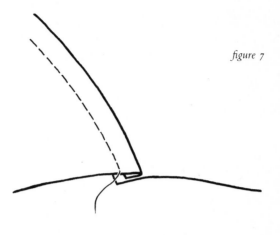

figure 7

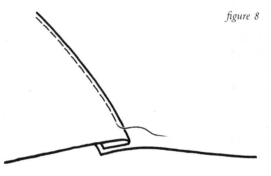

figure 8

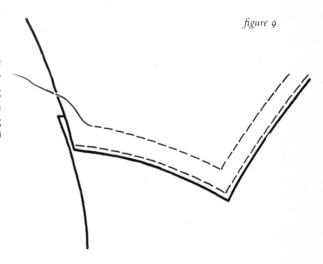

figure 9

Overlaid seam for thicker leathers

Here, no turnings are doubled under, so this seam is
suitable for harder leathers or suède splits. It will not
do for fake leather, where the cut edge should not
show. Allow a 1.2 cm ($\frac{1}{2}$ in.) turning on the underlap, but no turning at all on the overlap. First, stick
the seam with Copydex, with the overlap edge to
the seamline of the underlap. Top-stitch 3 mm
($\frac{1}{8}$ in.) in from the edge. Then stitch again, 1 cm
($\frac{3}{8}$ in.) inside the first machining, to catch in the
free edge of the underlap. Top-stitching is usually
on the forward side of the seam. Both these types
of overlaid seam are useful for curved or angled
seams. (*Figure 9*)

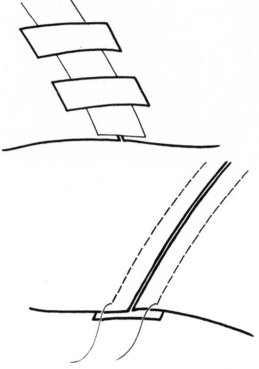

Slot seam

This is a good way of introducing contrast on thick
leathers, but is not suitable for fakes. Cut the backing strip 3 cm ($1\frac{1}{4}$ in.) wide. Match together the
edges of the garment pieces, wrong side up – lay the
strip wrong side up on top, keeping it centred over
the seam – and hold all together with Sellotape or
masking tape on the wrong side. Stitch from the
right side, keeping the lines of stitching 6 mm ($\frac{1}{4}$ in.)
or more from the slot. No seam allowance is needed
on either garment piece. (*Figure 10*)

figure 10

Strap seam

This is another good seam for introducing contrast,
especially leather contrast on suède, or for reptile
trim. First match the garment edges, right side up.
Then stick the strap over them, and top-stitch. No
seam allowances are needed. This seam is no stronger than the strap. Reptile, which splits rather
easily, should first be mounted on heavy interfacing, or on suède. (*Figure 11*)

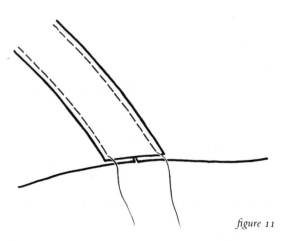

figure 11

Faggoted seam

In this seam, strips of leather are used like the rungs of a ladder, to join two garment panels. The effect is similar, on a much larger scale, to the faggoting stitch used as an insertion on fine fabrics. A faggoted seam can give an attractive lightness of style to a yoke or a pocket flap. *(Figure 12)*

Cut the strips no narrower than 6 mm ($\frac{1}{4}$ in.), because they must be wide enough to be held securely by the stitching at each end. Arrange them in a straight or diamond pattern, keeping them accurately spaced by laying them right side up over Sellotape. Place them so that they do not cross each other at the points where they will be stitched, otherwise the seam may become lumpy. Then bring up the two garment edges, place them level, and stick them with Copydex over the strip ends. If the garment edges are already turned under, simply machine close to each fold, and peel off the Sellotape from the wrong side. If you use a criss-cross pattern of strips, this plain edge is the easiest to keep regular. *(Figure 13)*

If you are using a firm leather, the edges of the seam would not be folded under. In this case, a narrow edging of leather, pinked along each side and top-stitched, makes a decorative finish. It can be used to great effect on curved seams, as the pinked edging will easily accommodate itself to a curve. Trim off the ends of the faggoting strips after stitching. *(Figure 14)*

Ridged seam

Here, the raw edges are finished on the right side. This seam is for heavy leathers only, particularly bovine splits. It gives a squared-up look to gored or panelled skirts. It is not suitable for fake leathers. Allow only 6 mm ($\frac{1}{4}$ in.) for each seam allowance, and stitch with a wide-set zig-zag right over the edge, or with a straight stitch a bare 6 mm in from the edge. Hold with hair-clips while stitching. *(Figure 15)*

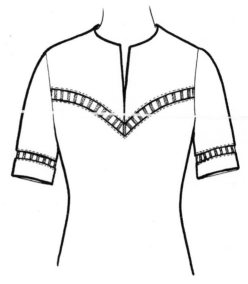

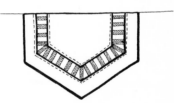

figure 12

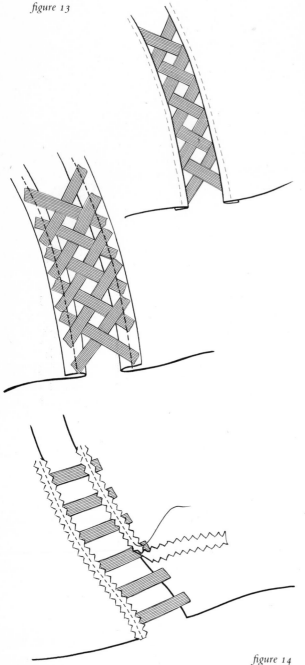

figure 13

Curved seams

Use the normal dressmaking methods to allow the turnings of curved seams to lie flat, cutting V shapes out of convex edges, or clipping concave ones. Stick in place and pound. This is useful, too, for collar edges – see page 58. *(Figure 16)*

Taped seams

Because leather stretches, particularly the finer suèdes and chamois, it is best to tape any seam that may take strain. Always tape shoulder seams and corners in seams; collar, pocket, neckline or facing edges where there is no interfacing; and waistline seams. Usually it is advisable to tape armholes. Simply lay a narrow tape over the seamline, and stitch it into the seam as you machine. *(Figure 17)*

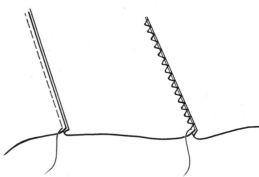

figure 15

figure 16

figure 14

46

FULLNESS

Darts

Avoid darts if possible. They do not look well in leather because it is difficult to make them lie properly flat at the point. It is better to turn a dart into a seam, as shown on page 30; both to give a smooth line and to economize in cutting out by using narrower panels. But if you *must* have darts, these are the alternative ways of neatening them:

Cut down the centre line of the dart, and overlap its edges. Stitch down the centre, from point to wide end, and tie off the ends of thread on the wrong side. Hold with a dot of adhesive. Trim off the wedge-shaped edges, leaving only 3 mm ($\frac{1}{8}$ in.) turnings on right and wrong sides. This is the better method for thick leathers. *(Figure 18)*

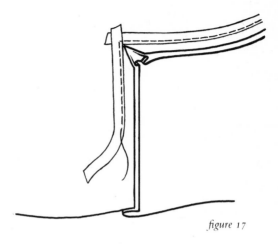

figure 17

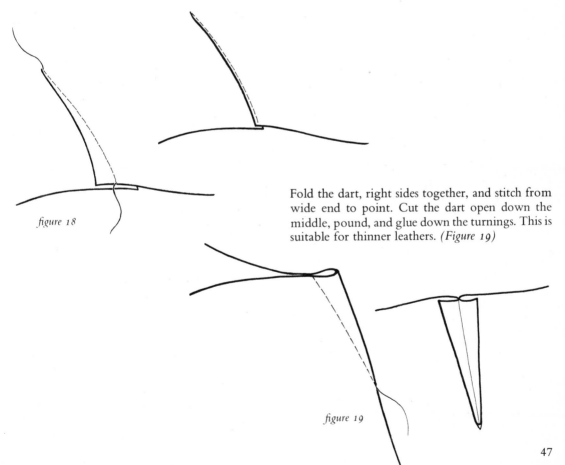

figure 18

Fold the dart, right sides together, and stitch from wide end to point. Cut the dart open down the middle, pound, and glue down the turnings. This is suitable for thinner leathers. *(Figure 19)*

figure 19

47

Tucks

Pin-tucks in suède and the finer nappas are simplicity itself to work. Set them no closer than 1 cm ($\frac{3}{8}$ in.) apart; a pin-tuck will take up 6 mm ($\frac{1}{4}$ in.), so you should allow that extra width for each one. Mark each end of the tuck, fold it right side out, and press the fold under brown paper. With the inner edge of the presser-foot as your guide, stitch 3 mm ($\frac{1}{8}$ in.) away from the fold. With a series of tucks, set about 1 cm apart, you may be able to keep them evenly spaced and parallel by letting the left-hand side of the presser-foot rest against the previous tuck, as you stitch. Lightly press all the tucks in the same direction. *(Figure 20)*

Tucked panels, such as pockets, should be tucked *before* cutting out. This makes it easier to get the tucks symmetrical. Left and right panels should be pressed so that the tucks lie in opposite directions. *(Figure 22)*

figure 20

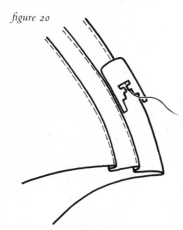

figure 22

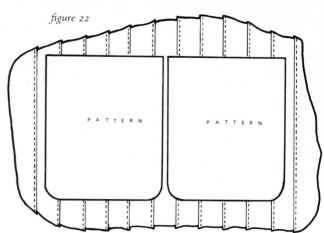

Tucks may also be stitched on the *wrong* side, when the natural resilience of the leather will give, on the right side, an effect like cartridge pleating. Do not press or pound. *(Figure 21)*

Gathers

Gathering is possible only on fine glove-weight nappa or suède, or on chamois. It gives a beautifully graceful line, particularly to a sleeve. This blouse was made in Pittard's washable gloving suède, 0.5 mm thick. *(Figure 23)*

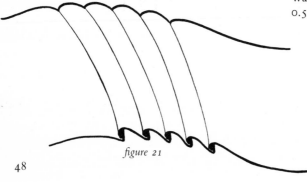

figure 21

Blouse made in Pittard's washable gloving suède.

figure 23

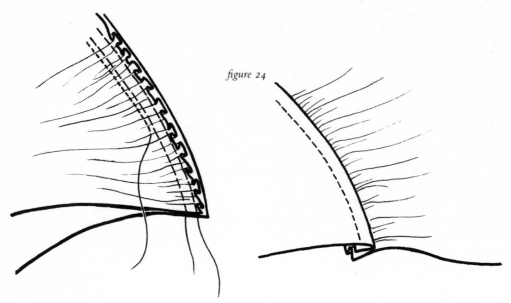

figure 24

Allow 1.2 cm (½ in.) turnings on both edges. Along the wider piece, run two gathering threads, one 6 mm (¼ in.) from the edge, and the other just inside the seam allowance. Use the very longest stitch you can set, and a strong thread. Draw up to fit, place right sides together and stitch the seam, hiding the gathering threads. Pound the turnings away from the gathered piece. Top-stitch 6 mm (¼ in.) away from the seamline, through both turnings, to hold them flat. *(Figure 24)*

Pleats

A knife, box or inverted pleat will set well in most leathers, except the very thickest. As in fabric, each pleat will take up three times its own width. It should be cut with seams at the inside of the pleat, so that smaller panels can be used. This also makes sure the pleat will lie flat. A box pleat has its seams at the centre; an inverted pleat, at the sides. *(Figure 25)*

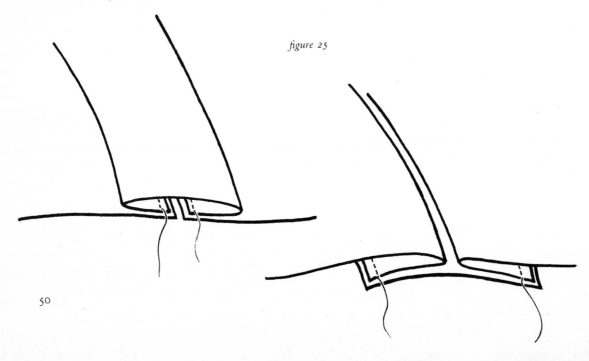

figure 25

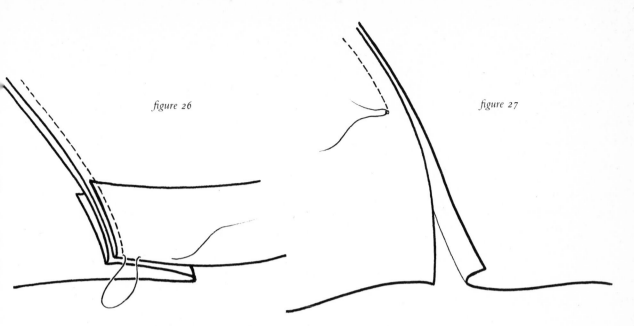

figure 26

figure 27

The folds should be kept sharp by pounding or pressing, and then laying a trace of adhesive along them, just in the crease. To finish the lower ends of pleats, first turn up and press or pound the hem of each piece, and secure with adhesive. Then stitch the seam at the back of the pleat, right down to the lower edge of the hem. Do not back-stitch, as this might weaken the seam; it is better to tie off the thread ends, put them into a needle, and thread them away inside the hem. Secure the knot with a dot of adhesive. *(Figure 26)*

Godets

Godets are long triangles let into seams. They give width like a pleat, but without bulk at the top. They can be pressed flat to look like pleats, but really look better, in leather, as flared panels, usually in a skirt.

First, stitch the seam from the top down to the level of the godet, tie off the ends of thread, and secure the knot with a little adhesive. *(Figure 27)*

Now, stitch the godet triangle, from point to lower edge, down one of its sides. *(Figure 28)*

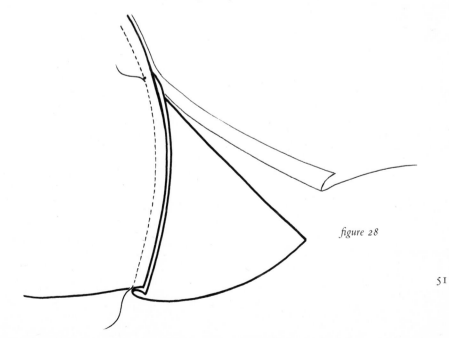

figure 28

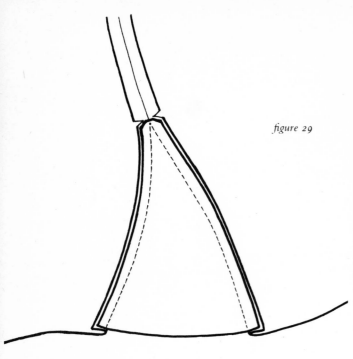

figure 29

Repeat with the other side. *(Figure 29)*

Trim the point of the godet, clip and pound the turnings, and top-stitch if liked.

INTERFACING

Leather needs interfacing to keep its shape, and prevent it from stretching. It is used in the same way as on fabric, and in the same areas. Do not use dyed interfacings, as they may leave a stain on light-coloured suède after cleaning. Different types of interfacing are used for different purposes:

Iron-on woven interfacings

These are for small or narrow areas, such as cuffs, collars, welts and waistbands. They are rarely needed in hems. They should not be carried through into seam turnings. Iron them on, without steam, and with the iron set at No 2, as for wool. Make sure that the bond is really firm, and then pound the edges of the interfacing.

Everbond Pinpoint 4/55, a calico with a fusible back, has been passed by the British Leather Manufacturers' Research Association as suitable for use in leather garments. It is quite heavy enough for most leathers. Only for the very heaviest garments will you need Everbond Pinpoint 21/55, which is a substantial canvas. (Everbond products are not obtainable retail. See list of Suppliers at the end of the book.)

If these are not available, use the fusible woven Moyceel or Staflex, stocked by good dress fabric departments. They are washable, but not guaranteed for dry-cleaning in leather. They also need rather more heat before the adhesive melts – or else steam, which one cannot use on leather. Do not be tempted to use the ordinary *non-woven* fusible interfacings. They have no 'give', and so may spoil the drape of the leather, and cause puckering. But the expansible Vilene, minutely slit all over to form a trellis, is suitable for leather.

Woven (non-stick) interfacings

These are suitable for strengthening the larger panels of a garment, such as across the back at shoulder level. This interfacing should be taken into the armhole seam only; at other seams it should be attached with a trace of adhesive just along the seamline. A light-weight, pre-shrunk calico is suitable for most leathers. For the finer ones, even a Terylene lawn may be enough. Do not use tailor's canvas, which is designed for dry-cleaning only, on a garment which could otherwise be washed.

Iron-on interfacing tape

Everbond Thermotape (safe for dry-cleaning or washing) is useful for bonding hems or strengthening facings seams. Also, of course, for holding down seam turnings. Just press the tape in place with a warm iron, peel off the backing paper, press the second layer of leather over the tape, and finish off by pounding.

LINING

Linings in leather clothes, as in fabric ones, help to keep a garment in shape, and to make it easier to slip on and off. A lining will also stop leather from clinging to the skin, and prevent the suède side from crocking – rubbing off in tiny fibres on other clothing. Linings should be cut out just as for cloth garments. Cut with 1.5 cm ($\frac{5}{8}$ in.) extra length, so that the lining does not pull at the hem; and allow for the usual pleat at the centre back of a jacket. In a skirt, keep the lining a fraction narrower than the leather measurement, to take the strain when sitting.

Lining fabrics

Choose the heaviest possible lining. It is a waste of time and effort to use the ordinary linings usually found in fabric departments, as they will not stand up to the wear in a leather garment. Use *either* a heavy triacetate or nylon poult, of dress weight, *or* a suit lining fabric, the heavy rayon satin used in good quality men's jackets. With the latter, though, there are two problems:

It frays abominably – you should machine zig-zag all round the pieces immediately after cutting out.

It must be ironed *quite dry*. The slightest spot of water will make a ring mark that is quite impossible to remove. This fabric is manufactured to be dry-cleaned in suits, so must never be allowed to come in contact with dampness, even from a steam iron, and certainly not be put into a washable garment. Apart from these points, it is a very satisfactory lining for heavier garments.

Methods of lining

There are three main ways of lining leather or suède garments. The tailoring method, used in the manufacture of leather coats and jackets, is described on page 86. But it might not be wise to attempt this on your first leather garment. The two following methods are more suitable, and considerably easier, for simple patterns and softer skins.

Lining sewn in by hand This method is best where there are leather facings round the neck, and at either the armhole (if sleeveless) or the lower end of the sleeve.

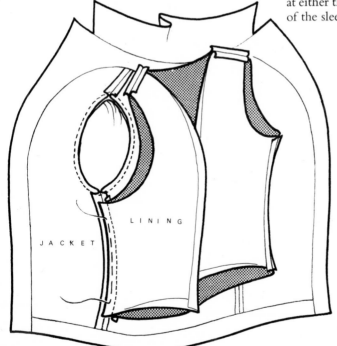

LINING

JACKET

figure 30

53

Make up the complete garment in leather, including any buttonholes.

Along the free edges of all the facings and hems, machine narrow corded braid, or bias-covered piping.

Make up the lining, complete except for the sleeves. Press all seams and darts.

Press under the seam allowances of the body lining, all round the neckline and fronts, and along the hem.

Lay the lining inside the garment, wrong sides together. Fold aside one lining front, so that you can tack together, or stick, the side seam turnings of the *lining* to the side seam turnings of the *leather*. (For clarity, the lining is here shown shortened.) *(Figure 30)*

Tack or stick together at the shoulder seams, in the same way, so that the lining is well anchored inside the garment.

Now fell the turned-in edges of the lining to the braid you have already attached round the facings and hem. It would be difficult to hand-stitch straight on to the leather, and the braid gives a couture finish to the edge of the lining. *(Figure 31)*

Stitch the seam of the sleeve linings, press, and keep the linings wrong side out. Turn the leather sleeves wrong side out, too. Match each lining to its sleeve, side by side, and tack or stick together their seam allowances, leaving just 5 cm (2 in.) free at both wrist and armhole ends. *(Figure 32)*

Slip your hand down inside the garment sleeve and draw its wrist end (and the wrist end of the lining too) back through to the right side. Turn in and fell the wrist end of the sleeve lining to the braid at the sleeve hem.

Turn in the seam allowance at the top end of the sleeve lining, and fell it in place over the lining at the armhole.

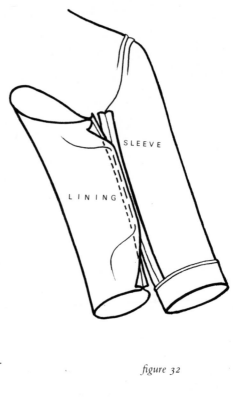

figure 32

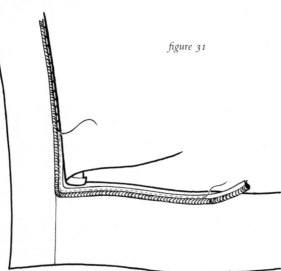

figure 31

Edge–to–edge lining In this method, the lining is cut from exactly the same pattern as the leather, except that a pleat may be laid down the centre back. It is suitable for sleeveless garments, and indeed for them it is by far the easiest and most satisfactory method. It is set in entirely by machine.

Stitch the shoulder seams, yoke seams, etc., of the leather, but *not* the side seams.

Do the same with the lining, again leaving the side seams open.

Place leather and lining *right* sides together, and machine right round the fronts, neck edge, and hems. Machine also round the armholes. *(Figure 33)*

Clip the seam turnings of curved seams, and trim corners.

Turn the garment right side out through the shoulders, pushing each front through one of the open seams in the back. Press lightly.

Stitch the side seams of the *leather*, making firm ends to these seams by beginning and ending a few stitches along on the lining. *(Figure 34)*

By hand, slip-stitch together the side seams of the lining, from its right side.

Top-stitch 1 cm ($\frac{3}{8}$ in.) from all the edges, to give a crisp finish, and to make sure that the lining does not show.

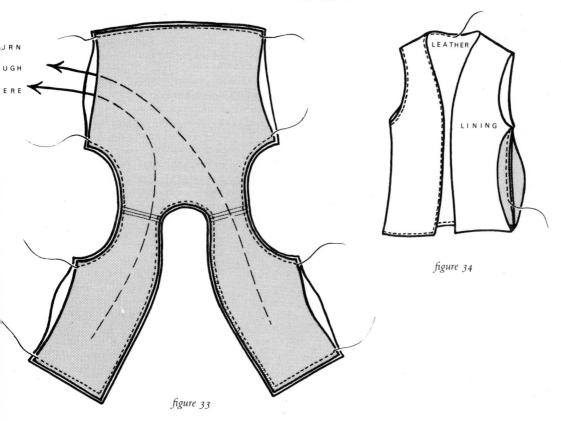

figure 33

figure 34

FACINGS

Facings are applied to leather garments in quite a different way from fabric ones. There is no problem of fraying at raw edges, and it is important to keep the number of thicknesses of leather to a minimum; so facings do not usually have their seam allowances turned in.

Turn in the *garment edge* first, press and stick it. At curves, clip or notch the turnings, as you would on fabric, to allow them to lie flat. Mitre at corners – the method is to pinch together the excess leather and trim it off, leaving no turning at the point of the corner itself, and no overlap of mitred edges. These are just butted together and stuck down. *(Figure 35)*

Stick the *facing* in place, with the full width of its seam allowances extending beyond the turned edges of the garment.

On the right side, top-stitch 3 mm ($\frac{1}{8}$ in.) from the garment edge, stitching the facing to it.

Trim off the seam allowance of the facing close to the stitching. This raw edge will just be hidden by the garment edge. *(Figure 36)*

On heavier leathers, it is even possible to dispense with the turning on the garment side. Waistcoat styles, for instance, in bovine nappa or suède split, can be cut without seam allowances at all, along faced edges. The facing is stuck in place, edges level, and top-stitched.

Facings can also be applied to the *right* side. (See page 94.) Both edges of the facing strip would then be top-stitched. This makes a splendid shirt-front finish. It is perhaps most effective if you use the reverse of the leather; for instance, grain-side facings on a suède garment – in this case, any collar, pocket flaps, etc., would also be made up on the grain side. *(Figure 37)*

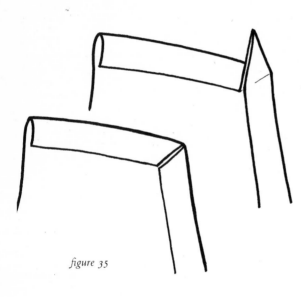

figure 35

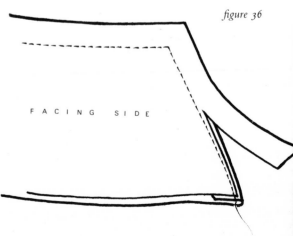

figure 36

FACING   SIDE

For inside facings also, the grain side is more satisfactory than the suède, because it allows the garment to be slipped on and off more easily, and because the suède side tends to ride up.

Fake leathers should show no raw edges, so facings must be turned, as in fabric, unless the top-stitching is set well back, about 6 mm ($\frac{1}{4}$ in.) from the edge, in which case the cut edge of the facing would not show. Good-quality mock suèdes, being of the same colour and texture throughout their thickness, can be treated as real suède.

Facings for sleeve openings are shown on page 63, and facings for tailored collars and revers, on page 86.

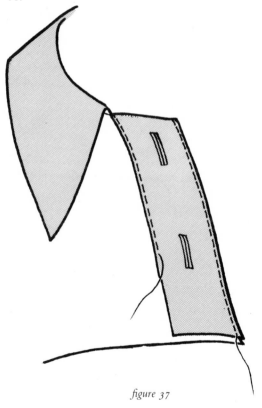

figure 37

COLLARS

Single-thickness collars are simple to make and apply; faced ones are a little more difficult.

Single-thickness collars

These can be edged in several different ways:
Notch the edge, turn it under, stick and pound. Top-stitching makes an effective finish, but is not essential. (See page 34.)

Bind the edge. (See page 93.)

Face the collar on the right side, with a matching or contrasting strip. (See the diagram on page 34.)

To attach a single-thickness collar, use a simple seam, with the *right* side of the collar placed to the *wrong* side of the garment. The turnings (on the right side, but hidden by the fall of the collar) can be pounded open, trimmed to 6 mm ($\frac{1}{4}$ in.) or less, and stuck down. This is a good method to use in open-necked styles, where the inside of the neckline may show below the collar. *(Figure 38)*

Alternatively, if the turnings are made to come on the *inside* of the neckline, they can be pounded downwards, away from the collar, top-stitched 6 mm ($\frac{1}{4}$ in.) below the seam, and trimmed to the top-stitching. Do not be afraid of close trimming in leather – the narrowness of the finished seam turnings is one of the main differences between dressmaking in leather and in fabric. *(Figure 39)*

Faced collars

These may be more substantial, and suitable for the more classic styles. Or they may, in thinner leather, still be soft and 'dressmaker' in effect, as on this navy-blue tunic, made in Pittard's brush-dyed gloving glacé. *(Figure 40)*

Apart from tailored collars, instructions for which are given on page 86, and fur-trimmed collars shown on page 84, here are two useful kinds.

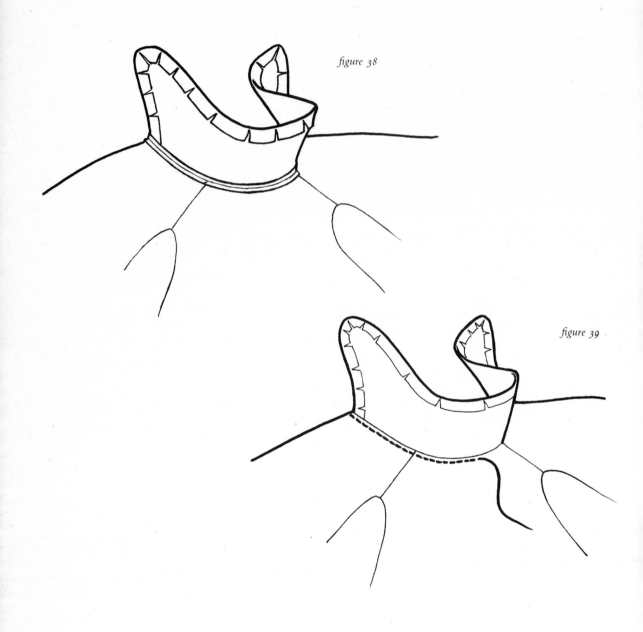

figure 38

figure 39

Right: Navy-blue tunic made in Pittard's brush-dyed
gloving glacé.

58

figure 40

The shirt collar

Apply in this way:

Stitch the under-collar to the garment, in a simple seam with the turnings *inside* the neckline. Pound them open, and stick.

Turn under and stick down the edges of the top collar. Stick it in place over the under-collar, moulding the roll of the collar as you go, and allowing the under-collar turnings to extend all round the free edges, as for facings – see page 56.

Top-stitch all round the free edges, and trim off the under-collar turnings right back to the top-stitching.

Now, on the *right* side of the garment, stitch exactly through the neckline seam of the under-collar, stitching in the neck edge of the top collar along its whole length. This seam could be held with staples before stitching. *(Figure 41)*

The mandarin collar

Use the same method for stand-up collars. These sit very well in leather, and should be interfaced. Here, it is the outer layer of collar that has its free edges turned; the inner layer of collar is trimmed. *(Figure 42)*

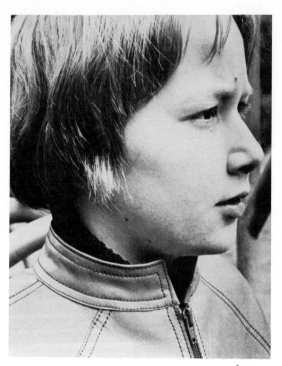

Mandarin collar.

figure 42

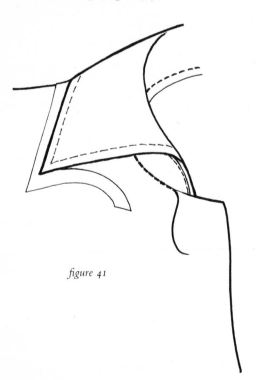

figure 41

SLEEVES

Treatment of sleeves depends, more than any other part of the garment, on the thickness of the leather. Gathers at sleevehead and cuff are splendid in gloving-weight leathers, or in chamois. In regular clothing-weight leathers they would present considerable difficulty and would look stiff and ungainly.

Set-in sleeves

The armhole seam should be taped, but otherwise is worked just as in fabric. In stiffer leathers, only the minimum of ease can be allowed at the sleevehead. Any extra can be reduced (as shown on page 30) or taken into darts – one of the few places in a leather garment where a dart may be necessary.

figure 43

Jacket made in Pittard's clothing grain, showing raglan sleeves.

Raglan sleeves

These are excellent on any weight of leather. You should consider carefully the type of seam to use, bearing in mind both the thickness of the leather, and how conspicuous a feature you want the seam to be. Raglan sleeve seams should be taped. Because of the width of these sleeves at the armhole, it is usually more economical to cut them in two parts, extending the usual shoulder dart into a full-length seam; as on this jacket, made in Pittard's clothing grain. *(Figure 43)*

Magyar sleeves

Particularly effective in the softer leathers. The seam below the shoulder-line takes less strain, so need not be taped. Magyar sleeves look their best on informal leisure clothes, such as this design for a man's jerkin in pigskin suède; or on dressmaker styles such as this one for gloving suède, with sharply-pressed grain-side pleating. *(Figure 44)*

Sleeve openings

Because of bulk, it is not possible to use the ordinary continuous-strip or shirt-sleeve openings. Instead, choose one of the following methods:

figure 44

The faced opening, suitable for thinner leathers. Stitch a rectangle of leather, right sides together, over the marking for the opening. Slash along the centre-line, layering the edge of the facing, and turn through to the wrong side. Pound the turned edges firmly, and stick down. You may find that top-stitching will add a crisper finish. (*Figure 45*)

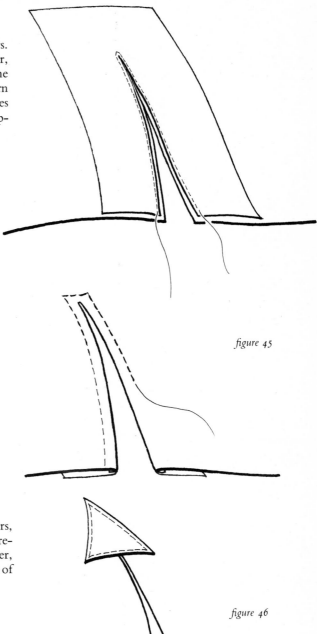

figure 45

The placket opening is better for thicker leathers, as it eliminates all bulk. Slash the opening, and re-inforce its point with an applied triangle of leather, stuck and top-stitched in place on the right side of the sleeve. (*Figure 46*)

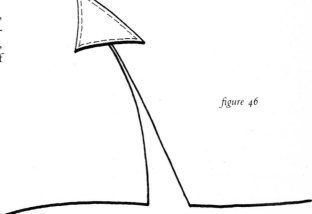

figure 46

Cuffs

To save leather, the sleeve does not usually extend down inside the cuff-band, but ends at its upper edge. The cuff therefore needs an interfacing, and also a facing, which is applied as described on page 56. It is stuck to the cuff near the seamline only; the upper edge of the cuff facing is left loose for attaching the lining.

For a gathered sleeve, apply the cuff-band just as you would a fabric one. The upper edge of the cuff facing is *not* turned in, though. It is either just stuck to the cuff and trimmed; or else top-stitched in place through the seam, and trimmed off close to the stitching. Always, when top-stitching through a previous seam, use the very longest stitch you can set. It will sink unobtrusively into the seam.

A third method of finishing a sleeve is with elastic or rib-knitted trim, about 5 cm (2 in.) wide. A contrasting colour, possibly with a contrasting zip also, might be considered. The edge of the trim is placed inside the sleeve, held stretched with Sellotape, and stitched sleeve-side up as an overlaid seam. *(Figure 47)*

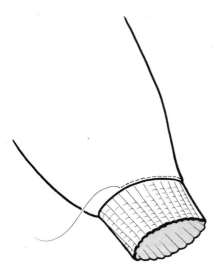

figure 47

POCKETS

Pockets can make or mar a garment. They are so conspicuous, particularly in leather, that they must be thought of as a principal feature of the design. The secret of success is to keep the pockets simple. Their proportion, placing and size are of far greater importance than elaborate detailing. It is vital that these be worked out on the cloth model, while you are actually trying it on. As pockets and flaps should be applied to the leather *before* the garment is made up, there is no later chance to experiment.

Slot pockets, often with flaps or welts, which look so well on manufactured leather clothes, are extremely testing to one's skill: if the leather is firm enough to support such pockets, then it will be too thick to allow you to handle easily all the layers. However, purely decorative welts or flaps over non-existent pockets are a much easier proposition; they set firmly and well because the leather beneath them has not been cut for a pocket placement. Equally, patch and seamline pockets are effective and simpler to work.

Flaps and welts

These are both made in the same way, with the edges turned in and the corners mitred. The facing is top-stitched in place, and trimmed to the stitching – as in the diagram on page 56. Alternatively, you could make a flap from a single thickness of leather, with the edges turned under and top-stitched. Welts, because of the strain likely to be put on them, need not only facing but interfacing.

When the welt or flap is made up, trim off the facing seam allowance along the unfinished edge, and attach to the garment by the seam allowance of the outer layer only. Place the flap or welt, upside down and right side towards the garment, with its seamline to the placement mark on the garment. Stitch the seam, tie off the thread ends and hold them with a dot of adhesive. Turn the flap down, and pound gently until it lies flat. *(Figure 48)*

Turn welts upwards, and top-stitch their ends to the garment. *(Figure 49)*

If the seam-turning is trimmed at the corners as shown, it will be quite hidden.

64

Flaps at yoke seams are perhaps the easiest to handle. Just make up the flap and include it in a seam, pound the seam turnings flat, and top-stitch, as in this design for a man's chamois pullover. *(Figure 50)*

Shoulder and cuff tabs are made in the same way, and taken into armhole or sleeve seams. *(Figure 51)*

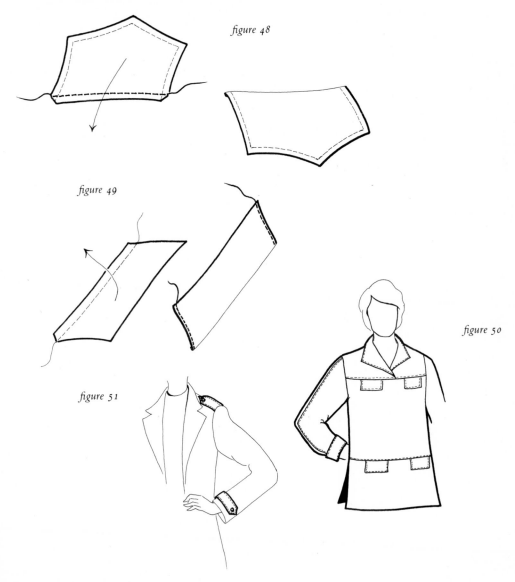

figure 48

figure 49

figure 50

figure 51

Unlined patch pockets

These may, but need not, be interfaced along their top edge. Cut the pocket with 1.2 cm (½ in.) turnings at sides and bottom, and a 4 cm (1½ in.) extension at the top to act as a facing. Turn in, notch and stick the side and bottom turnings. Turn in the facing extension, trim off the seam allowance at each end, stick down, and press or pound. (*Figure 52*)

The most satisfactory way to hold a pocket in place before stitching to the garment, is to stick it with Copydex along the edges to be stitched. Do not be tempted to use Sellotape on the right side, as it might lift the pigment from grain leather, or the nap from suède. On fake leathers, though, it might be safe. Try it first on a spare scrap.

Top-stitch the pocket in place 3 mm (⅛ in.) from the edges, beginning and ending with a small triangle of stitching, for strength. It is also a good policy to sew a small backing button behind each top pocket corner, as a reinforcement.

Patch pockets with flaps

Flap and pocket can be cut in one piece, without turnings, just folded and stitched as shown. Cut the leather the width, and up to twice the length, of the finished pocket. This will make quite a deep flap – but experiment in paper until you are satisfied with the proportions.

Crease the leather midway, *right* sides together, and press (A–A).

Crease again, 2.5 cm (1 in.) from the top edge, to the *wrong* side (B–B). (*Figure 53*)

figure 53

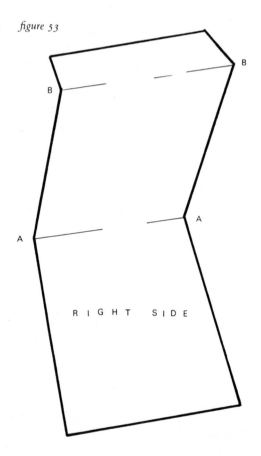

figure 52

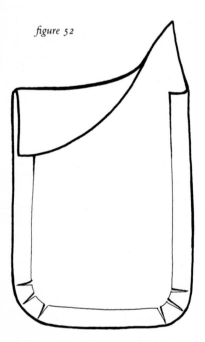

Place the wrong side of this crease to the wrong side of the first crease, and press the new fold (C–C), which will become the edge of the flap. *(Figure 54)*

Stick the two layers of the flap together, and top-stitch round the three sides of the flap, 3 mm ($\frac{1}{8}$ in.) from the edges (A–C–C–A).

Place the pocket in position and top-stitch to the garment, from B round the sides and bottom up to B again, catching into the seam the top inch of facing behind the pocket flap. *(Figure 55)*

Patch pockets can also be placed below yoke seams. Then their flaps can be made separately and in-cluded in the seams – as in this design for a suède shirt. *(Figure 56)*

Lined patch pockets

Cut the interfacing the finished size of the pocket. In the leather, allow turnings of 4 cm ($1\frac{1}{2}$ in.) for the facing extension, and 1.2 cm ($\frac{1}{2}$ in.) for the sides and bottom of the pocket. Cut the lining the same size, less 2.5 cm (1 in.) along the top. Iron the inter-facing to the wrong side of the pocket. *(Figure 57)*

Place the lining on the *right* side of the pocket, fold the facing over it, and stitch the seam round the sides. Notch and layer the turnings. *(Figure 58)*

Turn right side out through the opening, which is then stuck together with Copydex. Attach as before.

Zipped patch pockets

This is the simplest type of all, and very good looking. Having no turnings at all, it is particularly suitable for leather. First, set the zip into the pocket piece. Cut a slot 1 cm ($\frac{3}{8}$ in.) wide, and the length of the zip. Centre the zip under it, secure with masking tape on the wrong side, and stitch all round, overlapping the stitching at the end of the seam. (Figure 59) Then attach the pocket by machining 3 mm ($\frac{1}{8}$ in.) from its edges, all round.

The pocket of the boy's jacket on page 61 was made in this way.

figure 54

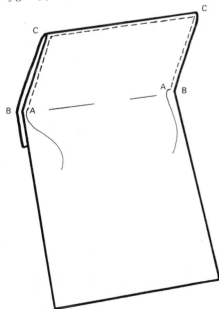

figure 55

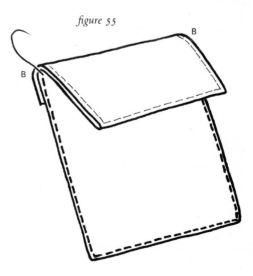

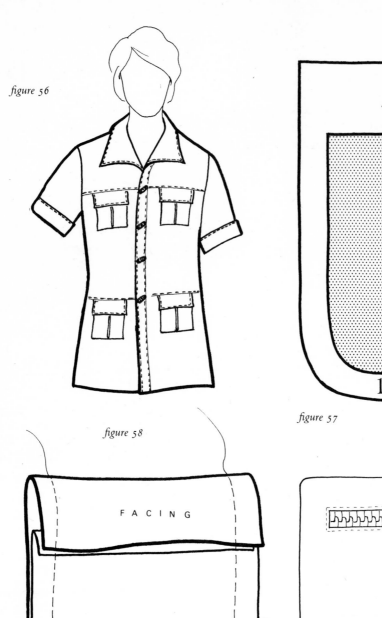

figure 56

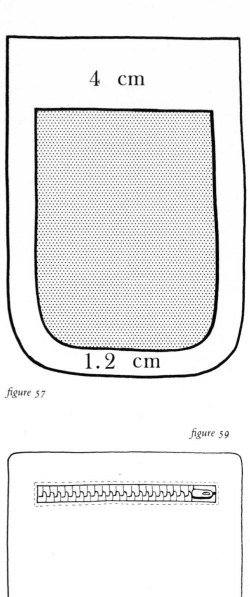

4 cm

1.2 cm

figure 57

figure 58

FACING

LINING

figure 59

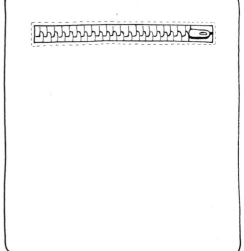

Patch pockets taken into seams

This kind of pocket, particularly if large and important, looks well on a skirt. Allow 1.2 cm ($\frac{1}{2}$ in.) turnings all round, and cut a shaped facing about 5 cm (2 in.) wide, for the opening. Attach the facing first. Then place the pocket so that it is level with the top and one edge of the skirt panel. Stitch in place along the bottom and side of the pocket. The free edges will then be taken into the side and waist seams when the skirt is made up. *(Figure 60)*

Pockets in yoke seams

These may be cut in one piece with the yoke and the lower bodice. To avoid stretching along the pocket mouth, it is as well to stick a strip of interfacing on the wrong side, along the front edge of the pocket. *(Figure 61)*

On the right side, the pocket would form an inconspicuous slit in the yoke seam. If the leather is at all thick, then the side of the pocket bag extending from the lower bodice piece could be replaced by a fabric lining.

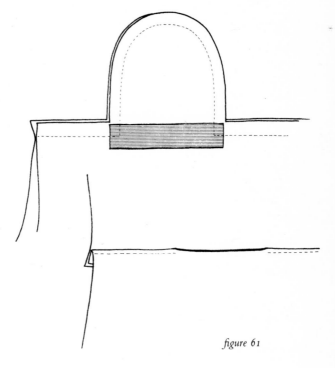

figure 61

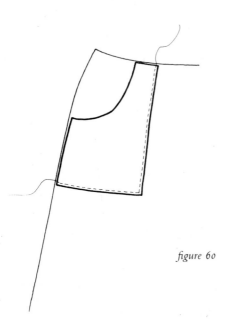

figure 60

69

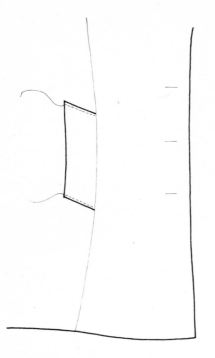

figure 62

Pockets in side seams

These are made in the same way as fabric ones. It is wise, though, to reinforce both edges of the pocket opening with iron-on interfacing strips. A welt may be incorporated without undue difficulty into a seamline pocket – a side-front seam is the most usual. It is applied in exactly the same way as a fabric one. *(Figure 62)*

When the seam has been stitched, including round the pocket bag, turn over to the right side, and pound the welt towards the side. Top-stitch its ends to the garment, and reinforce with backing buttons at the corners.

Slot pockets

These are not, perhaps, advisable on your first leather garment. In any case, it would be as well to make a practice pocket on a spare piece of leather, before tackling the real one. The size of the pocket is important. Allow the pocket mouth to be 4 cm ($1\frac{1}{2}$ in.) wider than the measurement across your hand, but no larger, or it may sag.

If there is a welt, then the front edge of the pocket bag will not show, and that half of the bag may be made from lining fabric.

Place the welt *below* the slot marking.

Over it, place one pocket half (lining).

Place the leather pocket half *above* the slot marking.

Stitch the slot seam along the upper and lower edges, 1 cm ($\frac{3}{8}$ in.) above and below the marking. Do *not* stitch across the ends. *(Figure 63)*

Cut along the slot, and clip the usual triangles at the corners.

Turn both pocket halves through to the wrong side. Turn the welt upwards.

Trim and layer the seam turnings, and stitch together the two halves of the pocket bag, catching in the little triangles of leather at each end of the slot.

Pound and stick down all leather turnings.

Top-stitch each end of the welt in place. *(Figure 64)*

If there is no welt, then the front edge of the pocket is formed by the upper part of the pocket lining; which must therefore have a leather facing not less than 5 cm (2 in.) wide. *(Figure 65)*

70

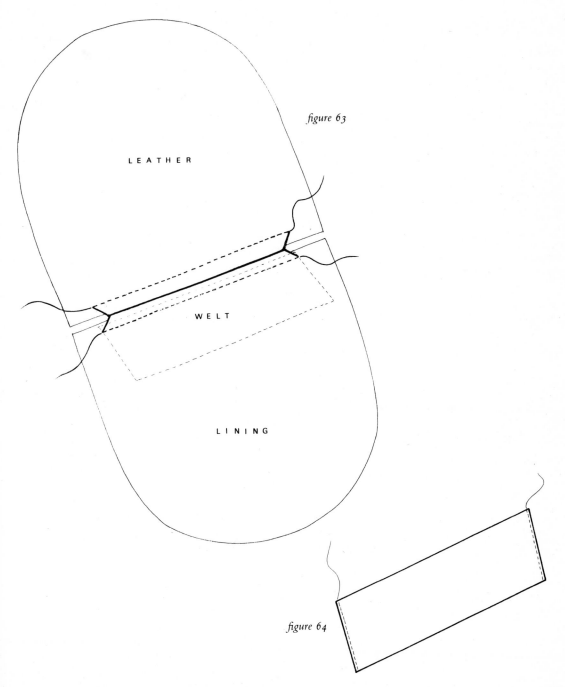

LEATHER

figure 63

WELT

LINING

figure 64

71

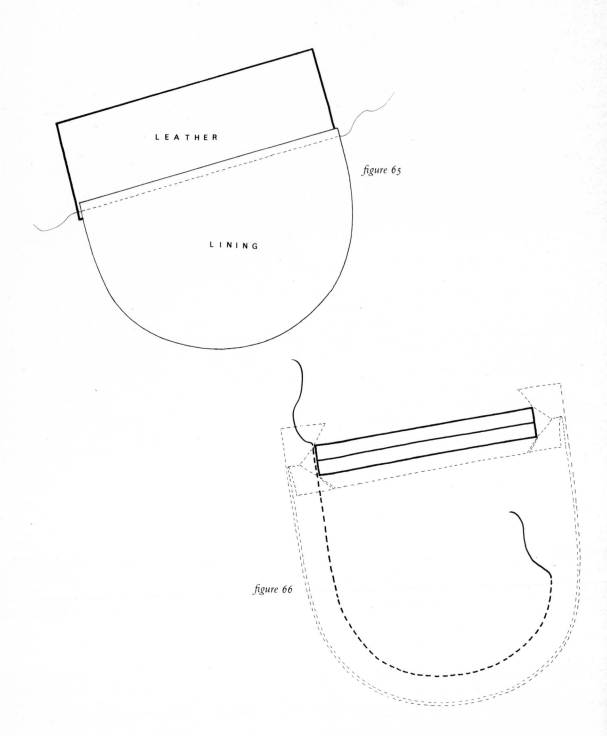

LEATHER

LINING

figure 65

figure 66

Waistcoat suit in bovine suède, split, machine
embroidered.

Cloak in bouclé, faced and strapped with hide grain
split.

Decorative facings and edge treatments. From top to bottom:

Gathering and flouncing on gloving nappa.
Machine embroidery on gloving nappa.
Chenille couching and suède appliqué on hide grain split.

Snakeskin and grain leather appliqué edging, on suède.
Couched braid and cut-outs on hide grain split, backed with suède.
Pinked, punched and studded facing of suède split.

When you turn the pocket through, allow the turnings along the lower edge of the slot to stand upwards. Lead the leather facing over them, fold down and pound to a good straight line, to show an even width of facing. Stick all these layers firmly together, and pound again, before machining the two halves of the pocket bag. In this diagram, the dotted lines show the construction and stitching on the *inside* of the garment. (*Figure 66*)

FASTENINGS

Zips

The smooth line given by a zip well suits the character of leather. See page 41 for the method of holding together the zip and the leather before stitching. Use only the heaviest-weight zips you can buy – metal, not nylon.

Whether or not seam turnings are made, depends on the thickness and handle of the leather; on firmer leathers, zips are better set against a flat, unturned edge – especially open-ended zips for cardigan and jerkin styles. In the lighter-weight leathers, turnings of 1 cm ($\frac{3}{8}$ in.) may be made, pressed and stuck down. For zips in slot openings, either cut the slot right out – or else slash the opening and clip into the corners, to make turnings of up to 1 cm ($\frac{3}{8}$ in.). (*Figure 67*)

Concealed zips for skirts and pants can be inserted with only a 6 mm ($\frac{1}{4}$ in.) unturned extension on the underlap edge, and a turning of 2.5 cm (1 in.) on the overlap. Any seam below the stop end of the zip should be taped. However, a zip will usually sit better in a straight centre-back seam than in a curved side seam. (*Figure 68*)

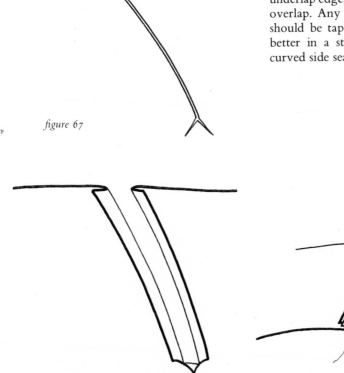

figure 67

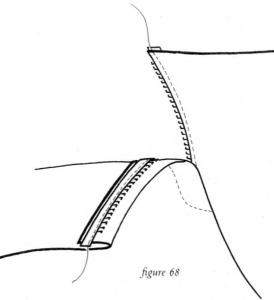

figure 68

Men's pullover designs may be difficult to slip on over the shoulders without straining the seams. An unconventional but effective solution is to insert a long zip down one side seam, from armhole to hem, set in upside-down with the opening end at the hem edge of the garment. The chamois windcheater and the minstrel's doublet shown in Plate 2 are both fastened in this way.

Velcro

Velcro is a godsend for casual leather clothes, particularly for children. It is suitable for any part of a garment – except where there may be considerable strain, such as a trouser waist fastening. The hooked side (which should be applied to face away from the body) will not scuff even the finest of suèdes. Apply by top-stitching round all four edges of the tape. As this can make an ugly rectangle of stitching on the right side, for instance on a front opening, it may be as well to design top-stitched detail as camouflage. *(Figure 69)*

BUTTONHOLES

On ready-made leather garments, particularly in the cheaper ranges, buttonholes are often machine-overlocked. These need to be worked on a buttonholing machine, as the ordinary buttonhole setting on a domestic machine is not satisfactory for leather. Neither, because of the difficulty of stitching, are hand-worked buttonholes. The kinds shown below are both easier to work and more suitable for leather.

Buttonholes in seams If you intend to fasten the garment by only one or two buttons, you may well be able to arrange your seams to accommodate buttonholes. To avoid strain on the leather, particularly at the end where the button will rest in wear, strengthen the seam turnings with interfacing. Stitch the seams, tie off and stick down the thread ends. *(Figure 70)*

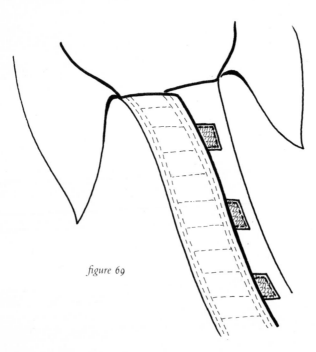

figure 69

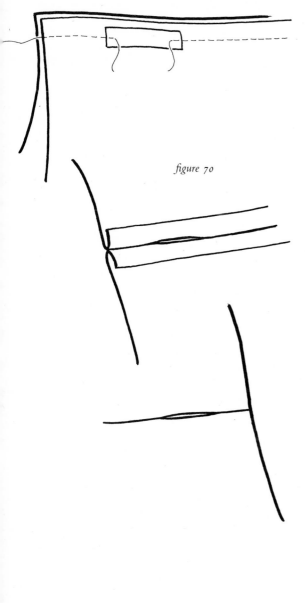

figure 70

Shirt-front buttonholes This utterly simple method is unique for leather, and cannot be worked on fabric. It looks best where there is an outside facing down a shirt opening, as in this design for a shirt-suède jacket. (*Figure 71*)

Mark the line and ends of each buttonhole with tailor's chalk. Top-stitch a rectangle 6 mm ($\frac{1}{4}$ in.) wide, and the length of the finished buttonhole, through both facing and garment. Slash the buttonhole midway between the stitching with a seam-ripper, working from ends to middle. That's all. (*Figure 72*)

figure 71

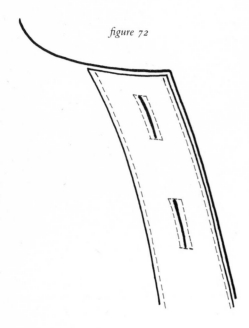

figure 72

Slash open, and clip into the corners, forming little triangles at each end. *(Figure 73)*

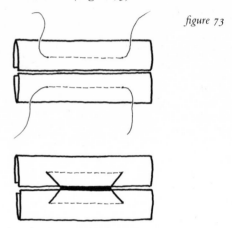

figure 73

Turn the two triangles and the two strips through to the wrong side, stick, and pound them. The two folded edges should meet precisely along the centre-line of the buttonhole. *(Figure 74)*

figure 74

Jetted buttonholes These give a classic finish on good-quality clothes. If you can make them in fabric, you should have no difficulty in leather. For the jetting, they need fine, supple leather taken from the belly part of the skin. They are worked before the facing is attached. The jetting should always show the grain side, even if you are working in suède, as it allows the button to slip through more easily.

For the jetting, cut strips of leather 2.5 cm (1 in.) longer than the finished buttonhole, and 2.5 cm wide.

Fold and stick the strips in half, right side outside, and place with their cut edges touching, one above and one below the buttonhole marking. They can be held in place with a line of Copydex, just along the centre line of the buttonhole. If any Copydex shows on completion of the buttonhole, just rub it off with a finger.

Stitch the two sides of the buttonhole exactly down the centre of each folded piece. Do *not* stitch the ends.

When the garment facing is finally stuck in place, top-stitch as shown, overlapping the ends of stitching. *(Figure 75)*

figure 75

Slit the facing with a seam-ripper, from the right side, and cutting from each end inwards. Then, on the wrong side, trim the facing to the stitching.

76

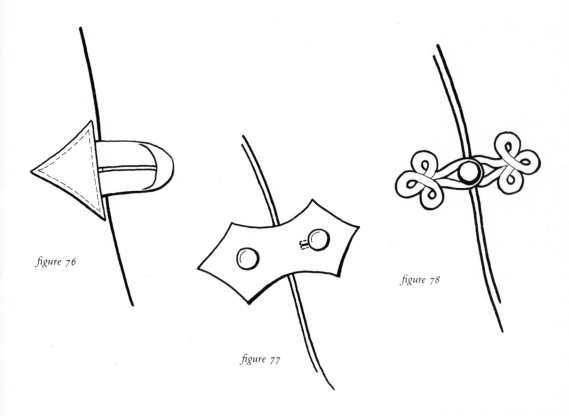

figure 76

figure 77

figure 78

Loop or strap buttonholes It is not always necessary to make buttonholes in the garment itself. They may be applied after the garment is finished. Some of the most effective designs for leather use straps, frogs or loops to hold the buttons or toggles. The fronts of the garment may overlap, or just meet edge to edge. The placing, number and proportions of the fastening you choose are of great importance, and should harmonize with the positions of seams and pockets. Loop buttonholes are secured to the garment with a top-stitched patch of leather, perhaps echoing the shape of a pocket-flap or collar point. The loop itself can be made simply from a strip of leather; or, if the garment leather does not seem strong enough for this purpose, a length of more substantial thonging could be used. *(Figure 76)*

Straps should be made in double thickness, with a shirt-front buttonhole at one or both ends. As well as for front fastenings, straps can be used to good effect to hold side seams in tabard-style garments – see page 84. *(Figure 77)*

Frogs can look very well on leather. The only difficulty is that they have to be sewn on by hand, using buttonhole twist. If you make your own frogs, use the thickest manageable cord, and roll the tightest possible loops. *(Figure 78)*

Buttons and toggles

Any kind of button may be used on leather, so long as you avoid a plastic that will not stand dry-cleaning, or a shank that is fixed on with a plastic cement. Horn or antler buttons, if you can get them, are splendid on outdoor garments. Perhaps the best, though, are leather-covered buttons made up over metal button-moulds. Use only the thinnest and most supple part of the skin, from the belly, to cover them; and make them on the hard-wearing grain side of the leather, as suède-covered buttons can soon look grubby. Toggles look well with either loop or frog fastenings. Under *all* buttons, sew a small backing button, to support the leather.

Lacings

Lacings are better for decoration or for a neckline, rather than for a full-length front opening. It can be a nuisance always to be slotting and unslotting a garment every time one puts it on or takes it off. The eyelets through which the lacing passes are applied with a die tool (supplied with the eyelets), or with special pliers. Experiment first to make sure that the eyelets hold firmly in double-thickness leather. Only purely decorative eyelets should be set into a single thickness. The lacing itself could be either a round silky cord or leather thonging, according to the style of the garment. Piping cord is also suitable.

Snap fasteners

These are applied in the same way as eyelet holes. They work well on ready-made clothes, where they are often used to avoid making buttonholes; but it is not easy to buy the larger and stronger sizes. The ones usually on sale in haberdashery departments are too small to make a firm closure. Mounted strips of press-studs, as sold for plackets, may be useful, though, for concealed fastenings.

WAIST FINISHES AND BELTS

Jacket waists

Waist seams are always taped for strength, and stuck open. Inset waistbands should be interfaced and faced. Layer the turnings, pound and stick them towards each other, inside the waistband. Stick on the waistband facing, top-stitch from the right side, and trim to the top-stitching. *(Figure 79)*

On skirts, a yoke facing applied on the right side can be an effective design feature. The yoke should have its waist edge turned in, and should be strengthened with tape stuck inside the fold. The skirt top edge needs no turning. *(Figure 81)*

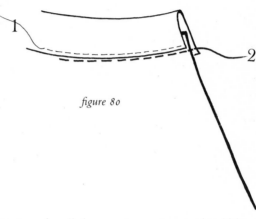

figure 80

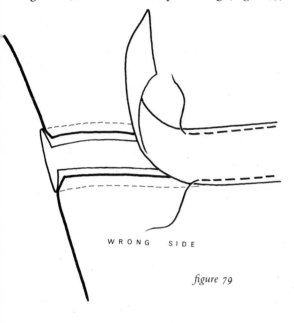

WRONG SIDE

figure 79

Facings for all these waist treatments should be of thin, supple leather, cut from a flanky part of the skin.

Belts

Belts are always made in double thickness, usually without turnings. Interface if you think the weight of the leather needs it. Stick on the facing, top-stitch from the right side, about 6 mm ($\frac{1}{4}$ in.) from the edges, and trim the facing to the stitching. *(Figure 82)*

Skirt and trouser waists

The waistline on such garments takes considerable strain. Therefore a petersham finish is not usually firm enough, unless turned in and top-stitched from the right side. Alternatively, make a regular waistband, finished with a large skirt-hook and bar. The waistband can be cut with its facing separate or in one piece. In either case, it should be interfaced. Stitch the waistband seam, either with a seam turning, or simply overlaid without turnings. The facing must *not* be turned in, but just laid behind the first seam, and top-stitched in place from the right side, close below the seamline. *(Figure 80)*

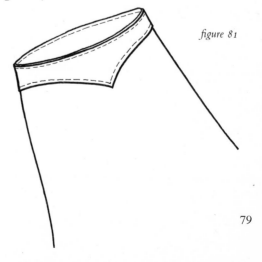

figure 81

79

At the buckle end, trim off a strip of facing, so that only one thickness of leather is threaded through the buckle. Prong-holes are best made with punch-pliers. See page 92. Or use eyelets if they will hold. A belt may sometimes, with very good effect, be replaced by a short buckled strap at the wasitline, perhaps taken into a side-front seam. (*Figure 83*)

Belts may also be made from plaited strips, or interlocked slotted pieces of leather. See page 100. Belt-carriers in thin leather may be made from folded strips, just stitched down the centre, and taken into side seams. In leather of any substance, however, these may prove to be rather awkward. A matching cord is easier to manage and looks neater.

HEMS

Hems on leather and suède should be from 1.5 to 4 cm ($\frac{5}{8}$ in. to $1\frac{1}{2}$ in.) deep; never more. The hem is just turned up, notched if flared, stuck and pounded.

Instead of Copydex, double-sided Sellotape or Scotch Tape may be used, or else iron-on Thermotape. Where a lining is to be attached, leave the top edge of the turning unstuck. Top-stitching may be worked if the design calls for it, though this is not necessary. Interfacing again is optional, depending on the weight of leather and the desired effect. It should seldom be needed.

In some cases, a cut edge may be left without a hem turning at all. A skirt, for instance, in bovine suède split is better without a turning, as also would be the edge of a very flared section such as a circular-cut peplum. See the blouse shown on page 49.

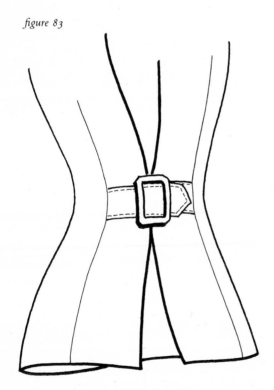

figure 83

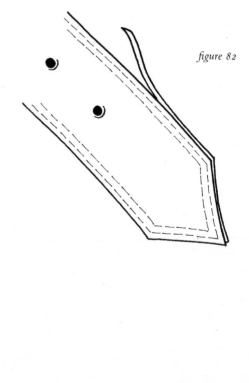

figure 82

SEWING FAKE LEATHER AND SUEDE

Fake leathers are usually composed of three layers, laminated together:

Vinyl or a similar surface material;

Foam in the middle of the sandwich, to give body and drape;

Backing fabric, which may be woven or a thin knit.

These laminated materials are treated according to their thickness and handle. Mostly, they are perfectly easy to control, as they are of uniform thickness and have little stretch.

Cut out with an ordinary fabric layout. It may or may not be necessary to observe the direction of the grain. Do not try to cut out in double thickness.

Trim and layer all seam turnings. Stick down where necessary.

If the cut edge shows up as a paler colour than the surface, then seam allowances in overlaid seams must be turned in and not trimmed off.

If the fake leather tends to stick as it is fed through the machine, dust lightly with talcum powder on the surface side. This can be brushed off later, quite easily, and will not clog the machine. Or use a Teflon foot.

Be very careful in using *any* heat on these fake leathers. Some may be safe for pressing, others may melt or go tacky, so you may not be able to use iron-on interfacings. Test first on a spare scrap.

To give ventilation in sleeved garments, always punch two or three holes through the leather, just below the armhole.

Fake suède differs from fake leathers in that it is homogeneous right through its thickness. The best quality is almost indistinguishable from real suède in surface texture, handle – and price. However, it is more economical to cut, being in ordinary fabric widths. It sews beautifully, with no problems.

SEWING SHEARLINGS

In making up shearlings, the skins need to be matched not only for texture and colour on the suède side, but also for the density, curl and colour of the wool. The direction in which the wool grows must also be taken into account. On the sheep, it runs from the neck towards the tail. In a garment, it should always go *down* the main body pieces. This is particularly important in sleeves, where the wool must run downwards from the sleevehead towards the wrist, otherwise any shirt or sweater will tend continually to ride up inside the shearling sleeve. Equally, in a shearling bonnet such as this one, the wool direction should be from front to back, so that the bonnet will stay snugly on the head, and not keep slipping backwards. *(Figure 84)*

figure 84

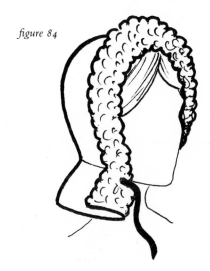

The main problem in making up shearlings is the bulkiness of the wool. Domestic sewing machines are not designed to cope with such a thickness. A dual-feed machine is really needed, with a wide measure of control over the pressure exerted as the garment passes under the foot. Without such a machine, *only the very simplest of garments should be attempted.* Here, however, are some ways in which handling difficulties can be kept to a minimum.

Shearling jacket by Richard Draper of Glastonbury.

figure 85

Seams

These types will avoid too much extra thickness along seamlines:

Overlaid seam Made without a turned edge. See page 44. First, trim the wool from the seam allowance of the overlap, with sharp scissors. Stitch the seam with the suède sides uppermost; place tissue paper under the garment as you stitch, to prevent the wool from dragging in the teeth of the machine. In some styles, such as the jacket shown here, the design calls for the woolled edge of the overlap to show along the seamline, in which case, the wool would not be trimmed off. However, the extra thickness in the seam would be more tricky to handle. This style is a good example of garments which need a specialist manufacturer's experience and equipment. Only the most skilled and intrepid of amateurs should attempt such garments. (*Figure 85*)

Overlocked seam With the wool sides together, sew with a wide zigzag, allowing the right-hand swing of the needle to take it beyond the edges of the suède. As you stitch, stroke the wool away between the two layers, with a ruler or paper-knife, to get a clean edge. This seam will pull almost flat in wear, and looks well on the suède side. It is invisible on the wool side.

Strap seam See page 44. The edges of the garment are just butted together, so that the seam is stitched through the strap and only one thickness of shearling at a time, making it much less bulky. This can be a very decorative design feature, with contrasting (perhaps patterned) strapping. But remember that the seam is only as strong as the strap.

Edge treatments

The garment edge may be turned under 1 cm ($\frac{3}{8}$ in.) and machined as a narrow hem. This is *not* easy to control, even if the wool is first trimmed away inside the fold. Another method is to trim the wool from the edge and apply a 3 cm ($1\frac{1}{4}$ in.) wide leather binding. See illustration on page 93. Where little strain will be placed on the edge, it could be finished simply by overlocking.

Fastenings

Buttonholes on shearlings present considerable difficulty. It is much more satisfactory to use either zips or buttoned-on leather strap fastenings. Buttonholes in these straps could be jetted, as shown on page 76, or the shirt-front type. (*Figure 86*)

ATTACHING FUR TO LEATHER

The sewing of fur demands completely different techniques from the sewing of leather. A separate book would be needed to do it justice. Here, instructions are given for one small aspect only – the attaching of fur trimming, such as a collar, to a leather garment.

As no seam turnings are made in fur, the very edge of the skin must coincide with the seamline.

Cut the fur, from the wrong side, *with a scalpel.* Keep the fur lifted slightly from the table surface, so that the scalpel cuts through the skin *only.* Pull the fur side gently apart without cutting through it at all.

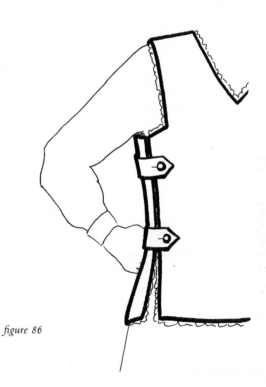

figure 86

84

Apply fur to a garment with the direction of the hair running downwards. This means that in a collar, for instance, there must be at least a centre-back seam in the fur; usually there will be several. Fur is sewn edge-to-edge, hair sides inside, with a close whip-stitch or blanket stitch. Stroke the fur away between the layers of skin, with the tip of your needle, as you sew.

As fur skins split easily, always mount them on a stay fabric, such as china silk or a fine lining. Mounting is worked, as on fabric, from the wrong side – by taking widely-spaced but tiny stitches through both the lining and the skin. Allow the stay fabric to extend 1 cm ($\frac{3}{8}$ in.) beyond the edges of the fur.

Strengthen all edges of the fur with tape. Overcast together the fur edge, the tape edge, and the *folded* edge of the stay fabric. *(Figure 87)*

When attaching a fur collar, make up the *under-collar* as part of the garment in the usual way; it should be of suède in a light enough weight to allow hand sewing round its edges.

Stitch the fur in place by hand. Slip-stitch to the under-collar just through the fold of the stay fabric, *not* through the edge of the fur itself. With your needle, stroke the hairs of the fur out of the way of the stitching, and hold them clear with your left thumb. The seam, although worked on the right side of the garment, will be entirely hidden by the fur.

The advantage of applying fur to leather in this way is that it can be removed when the garment is dry-cleaned, since fur and leather need different methods of cleaning.

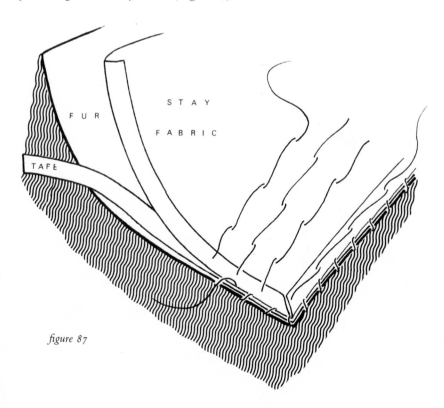

figure 87

Making a tailored jacket

A tailored jacket, with interfacing and lining, is not to be undertaken lightly. This is work needing some experience with leather. Tailoring is never easy; in leather, because one cannot shape the garment by steam and shrinking, even more skill is needed. But once one has become used to the feel of sewing leather, and has enough confidence to manipulate such awkward parts as collars and revers, then one can reasonably attempt a tailored jacket and expect to achieve a decent result.

These instructions are based on the methods used in manufacture, slightly adapted for the amateur with a domestic sewing machine. You may find the sequence of work surprising. The reason for taking the various steps in this order is to complete the entire garment and lining by machine.

Stitch darts, centre back seam and any yoke seams. Stick open and pound.

Make and stitch on any pockets.

Make jetted buttonholes as far as turning through. See page 76.

Stitch side, side-front and shoulder seams. Stick open and pound.

Turn up, press and stick the hem, leaving a loose edge 1.5 cm ($\frac{5}{8}$ in.) wide, to attach the lining.

Machine the under-collar to the jacket, clipping curves. Begin at the centre back, and machine up to the seam allowance at the side of the under-collar. Return to the centre back, and stitch to the other end of the under-collar. Clip and *pound open* the turnings from the step of the collar as far as the shoulder seam. Stick the turnings. Between the shoulder seams, clip and pound the turnings *towards the collar*, but do *not* stick them. *(Figure 1)*

Interface the leather front facings.

Machine leather front facings to lining fronts.

Stitch lining side and shoulder seams, to complete the body of the lining. Press the lining well now – you will not have another chance.

Interface the top collar. Make a coat-hanger loop.

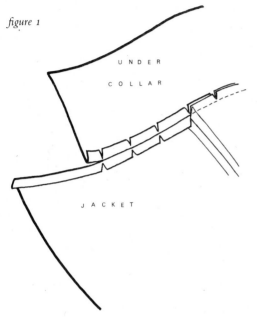

figure 1

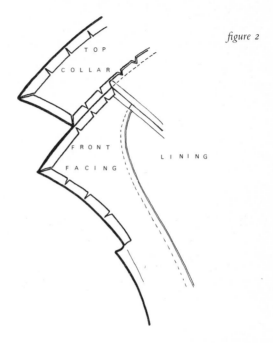

figure 2

Stitch the top collar to the lining, from shoulder to shoulder, taking the coat-hanger loop ends into the seam. Clip the turnings at the shoulder seams, and pound both edges together *towards the collar*. Do *not* stick.

Seam the top collar to the front facings, from shoulder seams to the step of the collar, where it joins the rever. Tape this seam. Do not continue the stitching into the seam allowance at the ends of the collar. Pound these turnings *open*, and stick.

Turn under, stick and pound the three free edges of the top collar. Mitre at the points of the collar, clipping off the excess so that the cut edges lie flat together, and are held down by adhesive.

Turn in, stick and pound the seam turning of the front facing from where it joins the top collar to the point of the rever. It is helpful to use adhesive tape to retain the shape of this edge, or to incorporate plain narrow tape, stuck just inside the fold of the leather. Mitre at the point, and continue turning in, taping and sticking the side of the rever down to the level of the top button. Clip and open out the turning there. *(Figure 2)*

On the *jacket front*, clip the seam allowance level with the top button. From there down to the hem, fold it in, tape, stick, and pound it in place. Trim the hem, as a mitre, to avoid an extra thickness of leather. *(Figure 3)*

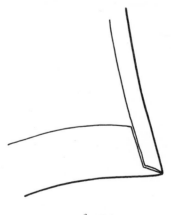

figure 3

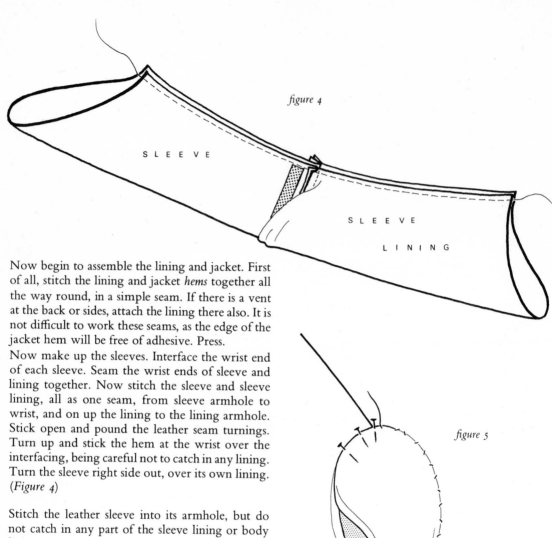

figure 4

figure 5

Now begin to assemble the lining and jacket. First of all, stitch the lining and jacket *hems* together all the way round, in a simple seam. If there is a vent at the back or sides, attach the lining there also. It is not difficult to work these seams, as the edge of the jacket hem will be free of adhesive. Press.

Now make up the sleeves. Interface the wrist end of each sleeve. Seam the wrist ends of sleeve and lining together. Now stitch the sleeve and sleeve lining, all as one seam, from sleeve armhole to wrist, and on up the lining to the lining armhole. Stick open and pound the leather seam turnings. Turn up and stick the hem at the wrist over the interfacing, being careful not to catch in any lining. Turn the sleeve right side out, over its own lining. *(Figure 4)*

Stitch the leather sleeve into its armhole, but do not catch in any part of the sleeve lining or body lining.

Now pin the sleeve lining in place over the body lining at the armhole, turning in the raw edges of the sleeve lining. Slip-baste just through the fold of the sleeve lining, and the single thickness of the jacket lining. *(Figure 5)*

Turn through to the wrong side of the lining, where the slip-basting will appear as a row of running stitches, just along the seamline. Beginning at the sleeve-head, machine right round the lining armhole. As the lining is not attached to the leather here, you will be able to manoeuvre it round quite easily to finish the seam. Repeat for the other sleeve.

Now you are ready to assemble the facings and top collar to the jacket. First, stick the top collar and under-collar together along their neckline, from shoulder to shoulder. All edges should be turned up towards the collar. If you prefer, these edges may be machined together, rather than stuck; this is standard practice in garment manufacture. Now, continue to stick the collar and under-collar seam turnings together, from the shoulder to the step of the collar. (They are opened out flat here.) Pound.

Then, beginning at the centre back of the collar, stick together the top and under-collar *edges*, letting the seam allowance of the under-collar extend outwards for the moment. Mould the roll of the collar as you go.

Stick together the revers and their facings, again letting the raw edge of the jacket rever extend beyond the folded edge of the rever facing. Continue down to the break at the level of the top button. *(Figure 6)*

Top-stitch from the level of the top button, up the rever, round the collar edge, and down the other side to top-button level again. This top-stitching should be 3 mm ($\frac{1}{8}$ in.) in from the folded edge. A second line of top-stitching should now be made, I cm ($\frac{3}{8}$ in.) inside the first, again to top-button level only.

Now stick the *lower* front edges to their facings, this time allowing the raw edge of the *facing* to extend beyond the folded edge of the jacket. At the hem, the facing is stuck *over* the hem. Top-stitch 3 mm ($\frac{1}{8}$ in.) from the edge, to complete the fronts. *(Figure 7)*

Carefully trim off all the raw edges, close to the top-stitching. These are shown here as shaded areas. Trim all the way round collar and revers, and down both front edges. The folded, stitched edge only will then be visible.

Now all that remains to be done is to finish the facings side of the buttonholes (see page 76), and sew on the buttons.

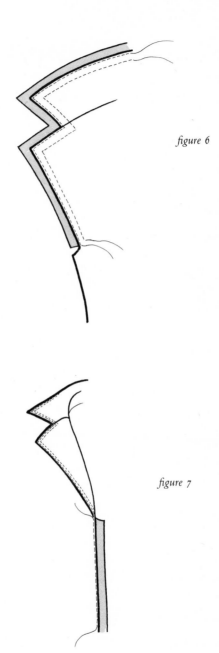

figure 6

figure 7

Decorating Leather

LEATHER WITH FABRICS

Beautiful as leather is by itself and unadorned, there is still great scope for designing garments which combine leather with other materials or contrasting textures. Knitted sleeves to suède waistcoats are a cliché, but suède seems to have a particular affinity with jersey of all weights. The gloving leathers look marvellous associated with fine polyester or silk jersey. Suède or grain leather strapping can give a bold line on the heavier double-knits, or on tweed or gaberdine. Strapping can also be used as a decorative facing on fabric, to hold the shape of an opening. *(Figure 1)*

Leather strapping used as a decorative facing on fabric.

figure 1

A superb and unexpected partner for leather is lace – try the thick cotton insertion lace, usually about 5 cm (2 in.) wide. It can be applied simply with buttonhole-twist top-stitching along each edge, leaving the leather intact behind it. Or, more dramatically, two panels of leather can be linked by a lace insertion, without any backing. This is perfectly feasible for vertical detailing on a bodice, in the same way as one might use rows of pin-tucks – or for horizontal insertion in full sleeves. It can be extraordinarily effective; and adds a bonus of coolness to leather evening wear. *(Figure 2)*

Panels of leather linked by a lace insertion.

figure 2

EDGE TREATMENTS

Although the following methods of dealing with edges are primarily decorative, they also serve a structural purpose in giving support and preventing stretch.

Fringeing

The simplest (but least attractive) method of fringeing is to mark, on the wrong side of the leather, the depth of the fringe; and to make parallel cuts not less than 3 mm ($\frac{1}{8}$ in.) apart, up to the mark.

Applying a separate fringe, however, gives a stronger finish, economizes in leather, and looks more interesting. Make the fringe on a 1 cm ($\frac{3}{8}$ in.) heading, place this inside the garment edge, and top-stitch. The fringe can, of course, be pieced along its heading, so that short lengths of leather can be used up. It can show the reverse of the leather, or even be of a different colour. An effective variant is to use folded strips of leather. *(Figure 3)*

Thonging

Thonging is simply an enlarged form of overcasting, worked through punched holes. In fabric, make the holes with a stiletto. In leather, use a pair of punch-pliers, that most efficient and indispensable tool, so well-designed for its purpose that it defies alteration or updating. Its revolving head can be set to punch six different hole sizes, and it works on all thicknesses of leather.

Thongs no narrower than 3 mm ($\frac{1}{8}$ in.) can be cut from the garment leather; or they can be bought in pre-cut lengths. If you want a contrast in colour, this would be the cheapest way of obtaining it.

Thonging can give a rather hard finish, more suitable perhaps for accessories than for garments. But try using instead a wider strip of soft nappa leather – about 1 cm ($\frac{3}{8}$ in.) wide; this will give a more feminine, 'dressmaker' effect. *(Figure 4)*

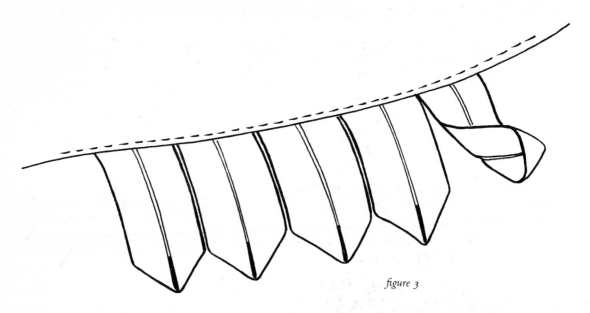

figure 3

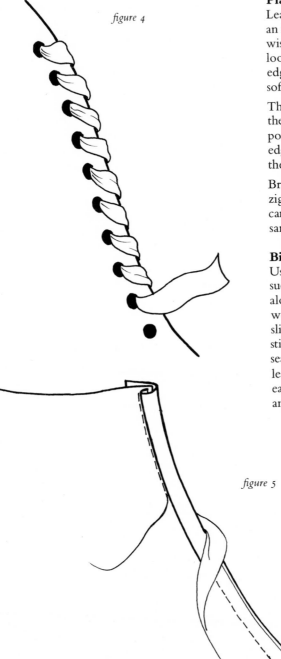

figure 4

Plaits and braids

Leather strips, plaited in three or four ply, can form an interesting edge finish. Do not pull them lengthwise as you plait, as this will give a thin, pinched look. Allow the strips to be half as long again as the edge to be trimmed, and let the plait settle into fat, soft lines.

The easiest way to apply a plaited edging is to run the machine, unthreaded but set at its longest possible stitch, 1 cm ($\frac{3}{8}$ in.) in from the garment edge. Then sew the plait in place by hand, through the machined holes.

Braid, of course, is simply machined on with a zigzag stitch along each of its edges. In this way, it can form an effective facing. Mitre at corners in the same way as for fabric.

Binding

Use strips of supple, flanky leather for binding. The suède side is not suitable, as it soon looks grubby along a front edge or cuff. Apply the binding as you would a fabric one, with right sides together; then slip the free edge, *unfolded*, to the inside, and topstitch it in place from the *right side*, just along the seamline. This is easiest with a zipper foot. As leather binding does not, like bias, adapt itself easily to curves, it is better used for straight edges and sharp, mitred corners. (*Figure 5*)

figure 5

Decorative facings

Facings applied to the right side of a leather garment provide an opportunity for great panache. As they will be the most eye-catching feature of the garment, it is important to plan their design and proportions from the outset, and work them out in detail on brown paper pinned to the cloth model. They can be straight; or shaped along their inner edge in any flowing or geometrical line you care to invent. There is no limit to the design possibilities. Here, the outlines have been adapted from heraldry. (*Figure 6*)

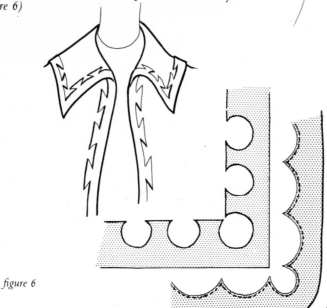

figure 6

The treatment of corners and curves is especially important. Start at a corner – where the front facing meets the hem, or at the point of the collar – and get the pattern right there first. The straight edges will then follow without trouble. Joins in the facing should also be planned. Skiving (see page 40) is useful here. The joins should be virtually invisible.

94

Facings on the right side are normally cut without turnings. This again gives added freedom to experiment with shapes. The reverse of the leather makes an excellent facing, particularly the grain side as a facing on suède, as it protects the garment edges from wear. Apply the facing by first sticking it in place, and then top-stitching along both edges.

Leather facings applied to fabric can be practical as well as decorative. The white bouclé evening cloak shown in Plate 3 has a hem faced with leather which will wipe clean, thus saving many trips to the dry-cleaner.

The facings themselves can be decorated in a number of ways. They can be pinked at the edges, punched with a design, embroidered, or decorated with studs. Cut-out patterns can possibly be backed by another colour, or edged with machine-couched cord. Some of these possibilities are shown in Plate 4.

LACINGS

Lacings can be functional, particularly at neckline openings, such as the chamois windcheater shown in Plate 2. Or they may be given a purely decorative rôle. Sleeves, for instance, made in two parts and laced from shoulder to wrist, are eye-catching. *(Figure 7)*

For a really exotic effect, the lacing itself can be 'embroidered'. Try working raised chain band over the horizontal bars of the lacing, using the next thinner gauge of cord. *(Figure 8)*

Lacings can also be used as part of the construction of a garment. See the slotted lacing of the cap shown on page 90.

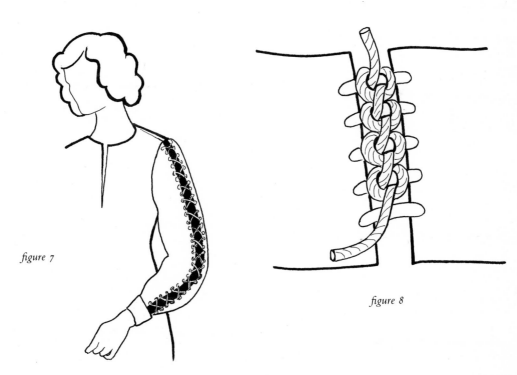

figure 7

figure 8

MACHINE EMBROIDERY ON LEATHER

Machine embroidery offers a most exciting range of possibilities with leather. In all decorative treatments, it is essential to practise on spare pieces of leather first, to make sure that the design is both effective and practicable on your particular leather.

Swing-needle machines give you a wide choice of stitches. Combine these into rich-looking border patterns for edges, straps or facings. Or try an all-over striped or chevron design as shown in the suit in Plate 3. Or you could use the machine for the appliqué of motifs or monograms. These should first be stuck on, and then sewn round their edges with a straight or zigzag stitch. Particularly effective can be shapes based on folded and cut paper designs, perhaps keeping the motifs the same size but varying the cut of each one, or perhaps repeating the same motif. (*Figures 9 and 9a*) Motifs can be of any size: the lion rampant on the Tudor minstrel's doublet in Plate 2, is 15 inches tall.

A further possibility is to use a twin-needle, with or without cord and cording-foot, to make a raised rib, in straight or curved lines. This technique can also create striking quilted patterns, with two thicknesses of leather or with a backing fabric. (*Figure 10*)

It is wise to make up the whole front or whole back of a garment, before working any all-over pattern. The design can then be chalked in on the right side, and worked right over the seams. It is usually best, though, to embroider a strap or facing before applying it to the garment. Then, you can work from the wrong side of the leather, using a thicker embroidery thread in the bobbin of the machine. Coton perlé, or even a bouclé thread, can be hand-wound on the bobbin; the needle-thread is not changed. Working from the wrong side, and using the swing-needle, you will produce on the right side a rich, crunchy texture, most striking on leather. (*Figure 11*)

figure 9

96

Spiral Page from The Book of Durrow; Seventh
Century illuminated Gospel Manuscript on parchment.
By courtesy of The Board of Trinity College, Dublin.

Chamois Windcheater with quilted yoke.

Tudor Minstrel's Doublet in clothing grain, with appliqué and slashing in suède. Photographed at The Porridge Pot, Warwick.

figure 9a

PAINTING ON LEATHER

It is tempting to try one's hand with acrylic paints, or even with felt-tips or heat-fixed crayons. Their colours stand out brilliantly, especially on the low-toned surface of suède.

There are, however, very real problems in the dry-cleaning or washing of painted leather. Be prepared for partial or total loss of the design in dry-cleaning. Hand-washing is better, though still not totally safe. The chrome-tanning process is designed, among other things, to make the surface of leather water-resistant and spongeable: in fact, to deter the adhesion of any outside substance. This is in contrast to bookbinding skivers, which are vegetable-tanned and treated to accept applied colour. Perhaps the only really satisfactory colouring agents to use on leather garments would be the old leather dyes, in their limited range of dark colours, or the aniline dyes and pigments used in the finishing of leather – but these are not easily available in small quantities.

If, however, you decide to take the risk – perhaps on an article that will not often be washed – then you will find the suède side will hold colour better than the grain side. Acrylic paints worked well into the surface in stencil patterns, seem to adhere best. 'Pentel' crayons, which are heat-set by pressing, adhere very well, but may lose some of their brightness after washing. Felt-tip colours survive dry-cleaning moderately well. Shoe-recolourants, of which there are several on the market, are opaque, pliable and effective; but they do rub off in creases, and are apt to disappear in dry-cleaning.

Quilted pattern formed by using a twin-needle.

figure 10

Rich decorative texture achieved by using
swing-needle stitches and embroidery thread.

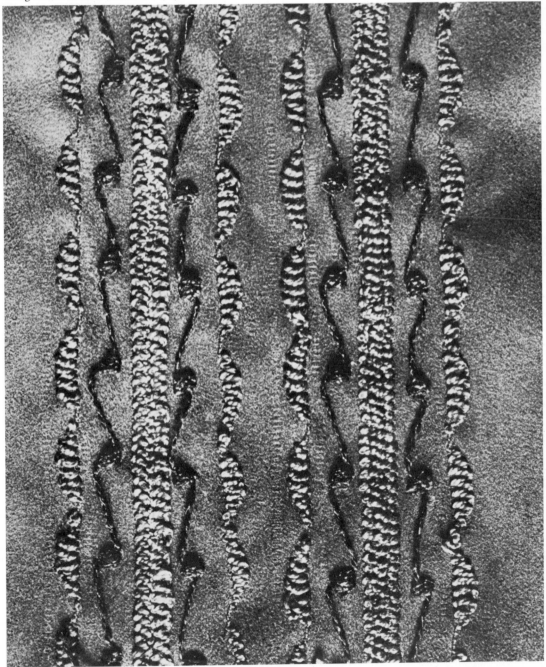

figure 11

SLOTTED LEATHER

Although belts and chokers made in this way have lately become somewhat commonplace, making them is none the less useful for learning how to cut and manipulate leather, and for making something out of small offcuts. A devious mother might use them to keep children from helping too enthusiastically with her own leather sewing. *(Figure 12)*

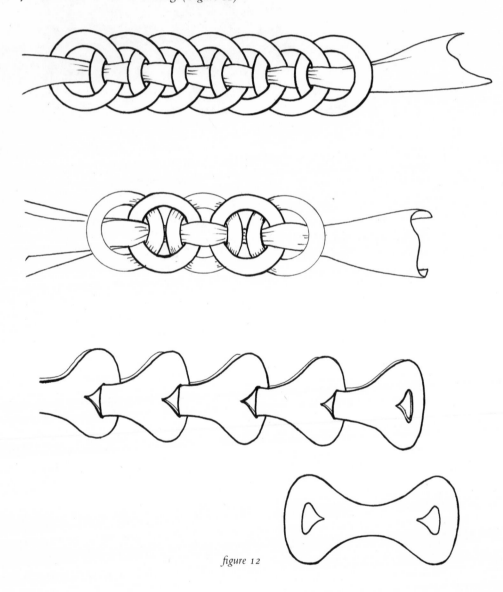

figure 12

LEATHER BEADS

The time-honoured method of making beads from strips of coloured paper, wound round a knitting needle and fixed with glue, can easily be adapted for leather. The basic shapes are oblong or triangular. The number of turns round the knitting needle will depend on the thickness of the leather and the fatness required in the bead. Dabs of Copydex will secure the leather as it is rolled. These beads can be lacquered. Clear nail varnish marries well with the surface dressing of leather. String them with other beads, for instance those made from exotic seeds or nuts. Sequins threaded ten or twenty together, to form flexible cylinders, look well interspersed between the larger beads. Another activity for children. *(Figure 13)*

LEATHER PATCHWORK

Patchwork in leather can look splendid, and is a great deal simpler to work than in fabric. The whole business of card templates and turnings for each patch is avoided, giving much more freedom in the use of shapes. You can employ the traditional diamond, church-window, hexagon or clamshell shapes. These are most effective when the pattern is kept simple and the patches fairly large thus allowing the leather to speak for itself. *(Figure 14)*

Use a metal or plastic template, as for ordinary patchwork, to ensure that the patches are identical. Or even cut one from thick card. Chalk round its edges to give the cutting lines. Leather is so accommodating that even a slightly irregular patch can still be pounded into shape and used.

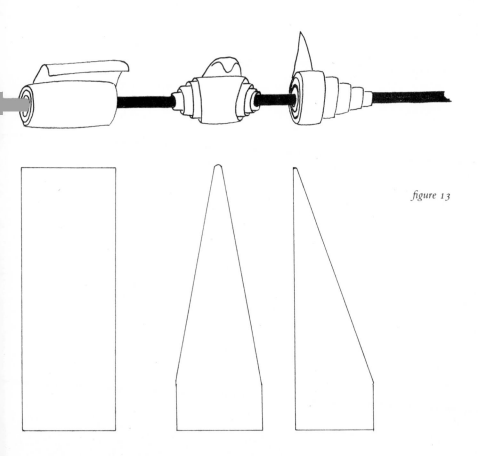

figure 13

figure 14

There are two methods. Hide splits are firm enough to be sewn with their edges just overlapped, with a straight or zigzag stitch. So long as the patches are of the same thickness, and have the same degree of stretch, patchwork made in this way can be used on its own, without backing on an interfacing fabric.

Usually, though, the scraps of leather will be of lighter weight and of varying thickness, possibly including pieces of snakeskin, etc. In this case, it is essential to mount them from the outset on fabric. Cut out the garment panels first, in the backing fabric. Arrange the patches on them, butted edge-to-edge; then stick them down and machine over both edges with a wide zigzag. Pull the thread ends through to the wrong side and hold with a dot of adhesive – quick and secure. Press the whole panel under brown paper. Lastly, make up the garment, lined if necessary. This makes much easier the placing of the patches and the balance of colour. It also gives a more even drape and better wear.

Crazy patchwork, using any shapes cut to fit each other, is also a possibility: here, it is essential to use a backing fabric. A more practical way – and possible without backing – is to make strips of rectangles, of the same width for each strip, but not necessarily of the same length. Then stitch together the strips along their sides. Cushions and bags are good uses for this type of patchwork. *(Figure 15)*

Also made by the strip method, but needing far more skilful planning, would be this long skirt with graduated patches, cut alternately from the suède and the grain side of the leather. *(Figure 16)*

Patchwork in association with plain leather is perhaps the most satisfying; for instance, as a yoke or for pockets – or make a patchwork waistcoat or skirt with plain leather facings on the right side.

figure 16

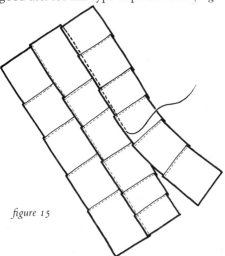

figure 15

Caring
for Leather

ROUTINE CARE

A grain leather garment should be put on its hanger while still warm from wearing, to allow creases to fall out. Do not put it away in a polythene bag. It needs ventilation, or it may become musty. Store it away from heat or damp.

Grain leather can be sponged, and rain spots simply wiped off. Occasionally, it may be fed with a proprietary leather dressing, such as 'Leather Groom' foam, and lightly polished with a soft cloth. White marks appearing underarm, caused by sweat, can be removed with white spirit – which is effective with most stains and quite safe to use on grain leathers.

Fake leather can be cleaned simply by wiping with a cloth wrung out in soap and warm water. It should be stored away from excessive heat, which might make it tacky, and extreme cold, which might cause cracking.

Suède should be brushed to remove finger-marks, or better still stroked over with another piece of suède. An ironing-mitt covered on one side with suède would be ideal for this purpose. Rain spots should be allowed to dry out naturally, when they can be removed with a soft gum eraser or by brushing. Suède-cleaning cloths, such as 'Swade Groom', are useful for all-over freshening and for removing greasy marks at necklines. One can also use block erasers, containing fine carborundum, to work off harder marks, including ballpoint ink. The trouble is that, working over a particular mark, one can remove some of the dye, especially from shearlings, and a bleached-looking patch may be as conspicuous as a dirty mark. One solution is to keep the treatment to as small an area as possible. For this, a pencil-shaped typewriting eraser is effective. Protective treatment, to prevent the surface of suède from absorbing dirt, can be given by aerosol preparations such as 'Swade Guard'.

A suède-split skirt that has seated can usually be helped back into its original shape by ironing, under brown paper – working inwards from the hem and side seams of the back panel.

WASHING

Gloving leathers are completely washable by hand. So is chamois. Use lukewarm water and a glove shampoo, and squeeze the water gently through the garment. Rinse well. Blot off surplus water with a towel, but do not twist the leather or roll it up tightly. Never spin-dry. Dry the garment *away from heat*, either flat on a towel, or on a padded hanger.

Before it is quite dry, manipulate the leather between your hands to soften it, as for gloves. This may need to be done more than once, as the garment becomes drier; and is crucial to restoring the softness and drape of the garment. When completely dry, and *not* before then, it can be pressed, with a cool iron and the greatest caution, through a layer of brown paper. A guaranteed-washable gloving nappa or suède should come up as new: the suède blouse shown on page 49 was washed several times before being photographed.

DRY CLEANING

Professional dry cleaning is now perfectly safe for any chrome-tanned grain leather or suède. The garment should come back looking in brand new condition, provided that it was not allowed to become ingrained with dirt before cleaning. Never let a leather garment get too dirty before sending it to the cleaner. The dirtier it is, the harder the treatment it has to be given to get it back to a wearable state, and it may lose its new look altogether.

The solvents used for cleaning leather are:

White spirit, kind to leather, but not totally effective.

Perchloroethylene, still a widely-used fluid, but one that can be a little harsh. After cleaning in this, a very few garments need to be re-sprayed with pigment. It is, therefore, unsuitable for garments which combine grain leather with suède, or grain leathers in several colours.

Solvent 113, a new and highly satisfactory solvent, more effective than white spirit and safer than 'perk'.

In proper professional cleaning, the linings are removed and cleaned separately from the garments. Grain leather is cleaned by hand, re-oiled, re-pigmented if necessary, and pressed. The lining is finally pressed and replaced.

Suède is given a gentle sand-blasting to remove hard stains. After cleaning in a fluid which will also contain fats, the suède will normally be hung for a day to absorb moisture, spotted, re-oiled, pressed, re-tinted if necessary and hand-brushed or rubbed with fine emery to raise the nap.

As there are so many more processes in the cleaning of leather, many of them needing skilled labour, it is necessarily more expensive than the cleaning of fabric; but if one looks after a garment carefully (and remembers, for instance, to wear an apron when frying chips), then cleaning should not often be needed.

Before handing in your garment to be cleaned, be sure to ask for a form of guarantee in case of an unsatisfactory result. Be extremely wary of any firm insisting that they clean garments at customer's risk only. Included in the list of suppliers at the end of the book is the name of a leading firm specializing in the cleaning of leather, which will accept garments by post.

MENDING

Surface snags and scratches on grain leather are best stuck down or filled with ordinary clear nail varnish. This has a good affinity with the nitro-cellulose used on the surface of garment leathers.

Tears in leather The least conspicuous treatment is to pound the edges of the tear so that they meet closely, and then iron a piece of fusible interfacing over the wrong side of the tear. It could do more harm than good to attempt stitching the edges together, and the mend would certainly show.

Holes in leather Always keep a spare scrap of leather in case you need to patch any garment you have made. Otherwise, it is most unlikely that you will get a match. In a bought garment, you may be able to take a small piece from inside the hem. Cut the hole to a clean circle or oval. Cut a patch the same size, matching the weight of the leather and any grain-direction that is discernible. Fit the patch into the hole, and pound from the wrong side. Iron a larger patch of fusible interfacing over the wrong side. Alternatively, use Bostik No 1 to secure the interfacing. For a really major disaster, consider covering up with appliqué, or with a new pocket.

Worn dye on suède or grain leathers can be re-touched quite satisfactorily in small areas with a matching felt-tip pen. This will actually stand up well to dry cleaning. Polish grain leather, after this treatment, with a little leather dressing, or brush up the nap of suède.

Re-buttoning Use linen button thread. Be sure to sew a backing button behind any replaced button, and work through the existing needle-punctures.

Re-pocketing Use the old pocket as a pattern. There may be a half-lining of leather inside the pocket – you may have to replace the lining attached to the outer edge of the pocket only. Seam the tops of the lining pieces to the edges of the leather inside the pocket opening. There will be room for this, even along a narrow leather turning, if you use a zipper foot on the machine. Then, folding the main part of the garment out of the way, stitch the seam round the pocket bag, starting and finishing level with the pocket opening. See the instructions on page 70.

Re-binding As it will not be possible to match old and new binding, it is better to remove all the binding and start again. Stitch the new binding 3 mm ($\frac{1}{8}$ in.) inside the original line, to hide the previous needle-punctures. For the method of binding, see page 93.

Split seams usually come at awkward places, such as under armholes, where they cannot be reached by machine. It is perfectly possible to re-stitch them by hand from the right side, using a heavy thread and the tailor's drawing stitch. *(Figure 1)*

Work, if you can, through the previous holes, taking successive stitches along alternate sides of the seam. Draw the thread up rather tightly.

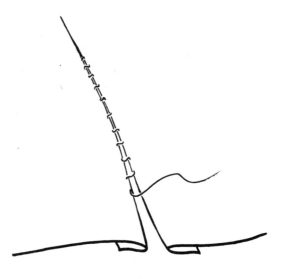

figure 1

RE-LINING A LEATHER JACKET

Leather coats last, with cleaning, almost indefinitely: their linings do not. A specialist dry cleaner will re-line a leather coat for you, but it is quite possible to do it yourself. You even have a perfectly-sized pattern already to hand, in the form of the old lining.

The pattern

Take out the old lining by unpicking at wrist, facings and hem. Do not cut off the seam turnings of the lining. The only place where you may need to cut the lining is along the back of the neck, between the shoulder seams. The lining is usually fitted inside the collar here – and it is not wise to take the collar to pieces.

Now unpick the whole lining, including the darts. Press the separate pieces, being careful to straighten out the seam turnings. Press along the thread of the fabric to get the true shape of the pieces. The marks of the old stitching will give you the fitting line for the new lining. Cut the turnings 1.5 cm ($\frac{5}{8}$ in.) outside these stitch-marks. At the back of the neck, where you have cut along the fitting line, you must also allow a 1.5 cm turning.

Lining fabrics

Choose the heaviest possible lining. It is a waste of time to use the ordinary linings found in fabric departments. They will not stand up to the wear in a leather garment. Use either a heavy triacetate or nylon poult of dress weight, or else a good quality rayon satin as used to line men's coats.

To work out how much lining you will need, measure the maximum length of the old front lining, and the length of the sleeve, including turnings. If the lining fabric is 135 cm (54 in.) or wider, then you will need to allow the length of the front lining plus the length of the sleeve, which may add up to about 1.60 metres (1$\frac{3}{4}$ yards). In fabric 90 cm (36 in.) or 115 cm (44 in.) wide, you will need *twice* the length of the front lining, plus the length of the sleeve, about 2.5 metres (2$\frac{3}{4}$ yards).

Cutting out

Fold the lining fabric in half, selvedges together, and right side inside. Use the old lining pieces as patterns, being careful to keep their grain straight with the grain of the new fabric. Place the centre back on a fold of the fabric. Mark darts, etc., with dressmaker's carbon paper or with tailor's tacks. Mark the width of the pleat down the centre back of the jacket lining, which gives ease of movement. Mark also the top of the back vent, if any. See how the sleeves were set in – were the sleeve-heads gathered or pleated into the armholes? Mark any pleats here.

Making up

When making and lining a new garment, all work is done by machine. However, when re-lining, some parts of the garment are not easy to reach by machine.

Re-lining by hand

The easiest way to re-line is first to make up the whole lining, sleeves and all, by machine. Press under the seam turnings all round the neck and facing edges, hem and cuffs – and then hand-fell these folded edges to the stitch-markings in the leather facings and hems. Use the same holes, both for ease of sewing and for neatness. This method, however, gives a less professional finish than inserting the lining by machine, so far as possible using factory methods.

Re-lining by machine

This is more difficult, but if you are an experienced dressmaker it will give a better result.

First, re-line the *pockets*, following the instructions on the opposite page.

Seam the lining *sleeves* from under-arm to wrist. If the sleeve is in two parts, stitch both seams. Press the turnings to one side. Match each lining to its own sleeve – the shaping shows clearly which is which. Pull the lining, wrong side out, up over the outside of each sleeve. At the wrist end, turn back the cuff to bring the raw edge of the leather facing to the outside. Level it with the edge of the lining (they will be right sides together), and also see that leather and lining match at the seams. Stitch by machine all round the wrist, keeping just within the original seamline to hide the previous stitching. Turn the lining to the inside of the sleeve, and leave it there for the moment, until you are ready to stitch the armholes.

Darts should be stitched next; usually the back shoulder darts and front shaping darts. Press in the pleat down the centre back, and tack across its top and bottom ends.

Match one *front facing* edge to its lining front, right sides together, and stitch by machine from shoulder down to hem, again keeping just within the original seamline. Repeat with the other front facing.

Now stitch the *shoulder seams* of the lining.

Fit the lining to the neck edge of the collar. This is the tricky part of fitting the lining, because when the jacket was first made, the lining would have gone up inside the neckline seam. However, it is not a good idea to un-stick or unpick the collar; so the next best thing is to stitch the lining across the back of the neckline, from shoulder seam to shoulder seam.

To do this, place the *right* side of the back lining to the jacket collar seam. At this point, the back lining will be upside down, extending *above* the jacket collar. Using a zipper foot, stitch lining and garment together, from one shoulder seam to the other, across the back of the neck, right up against the leather collar thicknesses. Fold the lining down inside the jacket; its neckline seam should now lie close against the inside of the collar. *(Figure 2)*

Stitch the *side seams* of the lining.

Pull each *sleeve lining* up, and pin in place over the body lining at the armhole. Slip-baste and work the armhole seams as shown on page 88. This is not difficult if the sleeve lining is pulled up well clear of the armhole.

Stitch the lining hem to the leather hem, right sides together, starting at one front, and leaving an opening of about 25 cm (10 in.) at the centre back, which will be completed by hand. (If there is a back vent, you need leave only the sides of the vent un-stitched.) Before turning the hem right side out, re-stick in place any leather turnings that may have come loose, using a little Copydex.

figure 2

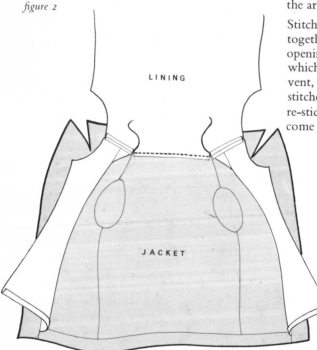

LINING

JACKET

Tanning your own wooled sheepskin

Tanning sheepskins is a cottage industry in some parts of the United Kingdom. It is perfectly possible to tan a raw skin straight from flaying. Be warned, though, that you will need plenty of space, under cover but open and well-ventilated, such as stabling, preferably with water and drainage. Tanning is messy, smelly and long – not an activity to be carried out indoors.

However, for the intrepid, the following is a recipe used in the Hebrides: one recommended in the woolskin-dressing courses organized by the Highlands and Islands Development Board. It produces sheepskins for rugs, etc., with firm, smooth pelts and wool as white as you could wish.

It is best to use a newly-flayed skin; but if you are not ready to start tanning at once, rub the flesh side with $\frac{1}{2}$ lb salt, fold the skin wool-side out, and you will be able to keep it in a cool place for a week or two, without putrefaction.

Steep the skin in cold water for a few hours to get rid of blood stains.

Rinse well, and wash in warm water and detergent. Ordinary washing-up liquid is suitable. Rinse well again. If there are brand-marks of tar or paint on the wool, remove them with acetone or a paint-stripper such as Polystrippa. Hang the skin over a line to drip out the weight of excess water. Do not allow it to dry right out, but just enough to handle easily.

Nail the skin, wool side down, on a board at least 3 feet by 4 feet. Use only *galvanized* nails: iron must never be allowed to come in contact with the tanning liquor, as together they cause a deep purple stain. Pull the skin out as tightly as possible, nailing the neck and tail ends close to their edges. Then pull out and nail the legs, then the belly sides. Make sure that every projecting part of the skin is held well stretched out with a nail. The process is similar to stretching and squaring-up an embroidery for mounting. Do not drive the nails right home, but just far enough to hold firmly. You may need to lift some of them to tighten the skin, and to inspect the wool side, during tanning. *(Figure 1)*

figure 1

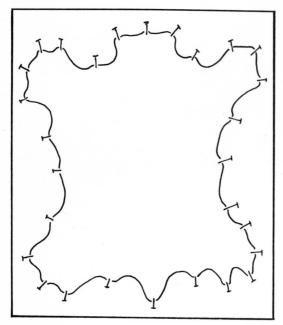

figure 2

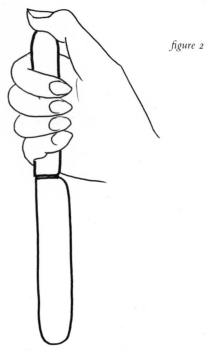

Now begin to break up the fat and fibres adhering to the skin. These must be scraped off, using a round-ended, blunt knife-blade. An old stainless-steel table-knife does very well. Work over the skin systematically and thoroughly with stabbing motions, holding the knife like a dagger, handle uppermost, with the blade slanting *towards* you. (*Figure 2*)

The fibres will not all come right off at once; this does not matter. The important thing is to break them up, so that the pickle and the tanning liquor can get through to the skin to do their work.

If the knife should make a hole right through the skin, sew it up at once with buttonhole-twist, just oversewing the edges or drawing them together with a stitch alternately over each edge. It will not show at all on the wool side. If you leave the hole, it will enlarge.

Make up the pickle, as a solution:

    1 lb potassium-aluminium-sulphate
    (potash alum)
    $\frac{1}{2}$ lb salt
    1 gallon water

Pour the solution on to the skin, and rub it in all over, taking care to treat thoroughly the neck, legs and all nailed-down edges. Massage the solution well into the skin, pressing especially hard with the heel of your hand. The solution is harmless to one's own skin, but if you can work as firmly in rubber gloves, they will prevent your hands from becoming too leathery.

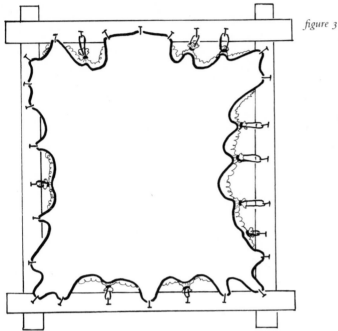

figure 3

Apply this alum solution three times a day for two days, each time working off any more pieces of fat and fibre that will come away – this becomes easier with each application of the pickle.

There is no need to rinse out the pickle. Carry straight on with the tanning. Use a liquor made up from:

4 lb Sheeptan
2 oz salt
4 oz chromium-potassium-sulphate
1 gallon water

To avoid any contact with iron, the solution must be mixed with a *wooden* or *plastic* spoon and kept in a *plastic* bucket. It froths on mixing, so use a good big bucket. Sheeptan is obtainable from the supplier listed at the end of this book. The other ingredients, for both pickle and tanning liquor, are obtainable from chemists, if given a few days' notice.

As with the pickle, pour on the tanning liquor and work it well in with your hands. Try to keep it from running over the edges of the skin, into the wool. If it does, it must be washed off later with warm water. Repeat this treatment three times a day until the liquor has gone right through the skin, all over. The thicker skin of the neck and shoulder takes longer for the liquor to penetrate; and the skin of an old ewe, longer than that of a lamb. Do not skimp on time. You may need three or four days. It is important that the skin should be thoroughly tanned. When the liquor has soaked right through, the skin on the wool side will have become a duck-egg bluish-green colour, definite and unmistakeable.

When you are satisfied that the tan is even all over, the skin should be taken off the board, and washed thoroughly in warm water and a mild detergent. The strong, oxygenated detergents, as used in washing machines, are not safe on leather. Neither are the biological washing powders; their enzymes will digest stains, and then go on to digest the leather – in fact removing much of the tannage. So use only a mild detergent, such as Stergene, designed for washing woollens by hand. The skin is then hung up to drip until it is nearly dry.

Now the skin must be stretched again, wool side down, on an open wooden frame; so that it can finish drying slowly, and in shape. Damp it lightly with water on the flesh side, if there are any dry patches. If it is dried out too quickly, it may crack, so never let it lie in the sun. Nail it to the frame; any parts that are too narrow or short to reach the frame should be tied with string and pulled out, to make the whole skin evenly taut. *(Figure 3)*

To give a supple leather, brush over the skin during drying a *little* sulphited sperm oil, diluted 1 part of oil to 3 parts of warm water. Too much oil may make the skin greasy.

If any patches of fat still adhere to the skin, mix some china clay powder with surgical spirit, and smear it on the skin. When this is dry and hard, scrape it off, and the traces of fat should be drawn out with it.

The skin should not be taken off the frame until it is totally dry. Then, work over the whole skin with a coarse grade of white sandpaper, wrapped round a small wooden block. Finish with a finer grade of sandpaper, to make a smooth nap. The skin may be rubbed down to whatever thickness is required. This also removes unevenly thick patches. So long as the surface is even all over, it is better not to take off much thickness. For a rug, the more substantial it is the better. Because of the length of wool, leather tanned by this method is really more suitable for such uses, than for even the simplest garments. However, it is possible to rub down the skin to whatever thinness you want, until it is manageable for hand-stitching or thonging – a square pouffe, or a cushion, would then be feasible. A collar might just be possible, attached as shown on page 84, but without a lining fabric.

Last of all, comb out the wool with a coarse-toothed metal comb, such as a dog comb, and trim off any ragged edges of skin. The wool may be given gloss by stroking it with a very little brilliantine.

The finished sheepskin can subsequently be dry-cleaned, or hand-washed and drip-dried. It should be shaken several times during drying, to restore the softness of the leather.

Suppliers

The suppliers listed overleaf are willing to accept small private orders or, where stated, orders from dress-making classes only. The minimum order would normally be one side of hide, or one skin, usually for cash on invoice.

CLOTHING LEATHERS

Barrow Hepburn Leather Store,
205 Kensington High Street,
London w8.

Clothing grain and suède, chamois, reptile skins. Tools, dyes and fittings.

C.W. Pittard & Co. Ltd,
Sherborne Road,
Yeovil,
Somerset.

Clothing grain and suède, and gloving suède and glacé, in a wide range of good colours. Samples and price list.

The Tannery Shop,
Gomshall Tanneries,
Queen Street,
Gomshall, Surrey.

Clothing nappa and suède in good colours. Washable suède. Bundles of offcuts. Catalogue with samples.

David E. Jacobs Ltd,
263–265 Hackney Road,
London E2.

Specialists in pigskin suède, supplied in a wide range of colours, in standard weight, 0.9 mm, and a lighter weight, 0.7 mm, with soft drape. Cow nappa sides and splits in a variety of colours. Aniline finish vealskins. Samples.

Strong & Fisher, Ltd,
Rushden,
Northants.

Suède and grain clothing leathers. Suèdalope in wide range of brilliant and pastel colours. Will supply authorized dressmaking classes. Sample swatches.

Connolly Bros (Curriers) Ltd,
39–43 Chalton Street,
Euston Road,
London NW1

Clothing leather sides and suède butt splits. Colours dependent on current production. These suède splits are the most economical leathers to buy.

G. Tanners Ltd,
Bridgehaugh Mill,
Selkirk,
Scotland.

Clothing pigskin, both suèded and grained. Suèded pigskin splits.

J.T. Batchelor & Co.,
39 Netherhall Gardens,
Hampstead,
London NW3

Clothing leathers, including suède and nappa; hides, python. Belt and handicraft leathers. Tools and fittings. Mail order only; 18p for list.

Rookes Leather Stores,
Clemens Street,
Leamington Spa.

Garment and handbag leathers. Whole skins or offcuts. Will order for customers' requirements.

John P. Milner, Ltd,
67 Queen Street,
Hitchin, Herts.

Clothing, glove and bag leathers. Linings, threads, tools and fixtures.

R. & A. Kohnstamm Ltd,
Croydon Road,
Beckenham,
Kent.

Factory and warehouse. Clothing grain and suède leathers. Open to the public only for leather sales, held several times a year; dates from mailing lists.

C. & D. Hudson
3 Roland Way,
Higham Ferrers,
Wellingborough, Northants.

Bags of pieces, (mixed colours), upholstery hide, woolled sheepskin, suède and grain clothing leathers, chamois. Mail order only. Price list.

Dryad,
Northgates,
Leicester.

Handicraft leathers, tools. Retail shop, not open on Saturdays. Catalogue and mail order.

SKINS FOR TRIMMING

A.T. Kinswood & Co. Ltd,
Enterprise Way,
Grovebury Road,
Leighton Buzzard, Beds.

Reptile skins for trimmings. Whip-snake, lizard, crocodile, emu, etc. Also diamond patchwork panels, 45 cm by 90 cm, in snakeskins. Wholesale only, to dressmaking classes.

Louis Grossé,
36 Manchester Street, London W1

Gold and silver kid.

WOOLLED SHEEPSKINS

Tescan,
Glastonbury,
Somerset.

Woolled sheepskins. Wolfix in various finishes. (Tescan is the Skin Sales Division of Clark, Son & Morland.)

CHAMOIS

J. & T. Beaven Ltd,
Holt,
Trowbridge,
Wilts.

Full oil-dressed chamois leather wholeskins, any quantity.

County Chamois Co. Ltd,
John Street Leather Works,
Glascote,
Tamworth,
Staffs.

Chamois wholeskins up to largest sizes. Minimum of six skins.

Edward Cope & Son Ltd,
Croft Tannery,
Westfields Avenue,
Higham Ferrers,
Wellingborough, Northants.

Small wholeskin chamois leathers (size 26 in. by 21 in.) supplied in lots of ten.

INTERFACINGS

J. Meggitt & Sons,
Cheetham Hill Road,
Cheetham Hill,
Manchester.

Woven fusible interfacings. Everbond Pinpoint 4/55 for most purposes. Everbond Pinpoint 21/55 for the heaviest applications. Both 90 cm wide. Also Everbond Thermotape, 10 mm, fusible on both sides.

FITTINGS

Rose (Fittings) Ltd,
337 City Road,
London EC1

Specialists in accessories and fittings for leather goods and clothing. Buckles, zips, eyelets, ornaments, chains, threads. Also mail order.

DRY CLEANERS

Westmans of Somerset,
Love Lane,
Burnham-on-Sea,
Somerset.

Specialist dry cleaners of grain leather and suède garments. Postal service.

TANNING SUPPLIES

Hodgson Tanning Products,
P.O. Box 5,
Beverley,
North Humberside.

Supplier of Sheeptan, mentioned on page 111. Also Sheepchrome (a mixture of Sheeptan and chrome powder). Sulphited oil.

Edward Wilson,
Aintree Road,
Bootle, Liverpool 20.

Toggles, knives, tools, etc. for woolskin processing.

Snowdonia Taxidermy Studios,
Fron Ganol,
School Bank Road,
Llanrwst,
Gwynedd,
N. Wales.

Home tanning kit, K-Tan, with instructions for tanning any wool or hair skin up to deer or large sheep, for rugs, etc. Offcuts of skins.

Index